The
SANE
CITIZENS
Political Handbook

The
SANE
CITIZENS
Political Handbook

ALEXANDER AND
ZACHARIAH OAKES

This book is dedicated to our parents, Howard and Deborah, who, for better or worse created a couple of freethinking Neanderthals who love liberty. Sincerely, thank you.

Contents

Foreword
By John Kinsman

I first "met" Alex while serving time in Bare Hill Correctional Facility for a crime that, to this day, I still feel I never should have served even 1 day for. That's relevant to this book because, preceding this stint in Bare Hill, a time when most of the mainstream media on both sides were hyper-focused on my case, I found it amazing how just mentioning my name whipped up a partisan-fueled frenzy of emotion in anybody even mildly familiar with me. This is to say that everybody on the opposite side of the political aisle was convinced that I was a racist Nazi, and many demanded no less than death for me, AND my family. Even worse, though I had never talked to these people, and even though they knew nothing of my family, when they discovered that I had a black wife and three mixed-race children, no, they didn't retract their statements, but rather they wrote entire articles and recorded full podcasts analyzing and/or hypothesizing about how brainwashed my wife was for marrying a racist; and how messed up my kids must be for being the brown offspring of a demonic racist who hates them. In other words, at no point did they consider the possibility that maybe, just maybe, I'm not racist at all.

During this experience I was shocked to see how many people could hate a person so much without knowing anything about them. You see, to them it was as simple as knowing that, politically speaking, I was a member of the "other team," and therefore evil. Anyway, as I make my way through the aftermath of this devastating chain of events, events that my family has still not fully recovered from, I am left to wonder, how did it get this bad? I mean, really, how the hell did we get to a place where society's extreme political passions, as well as an inability to listen to another person without considering what political party they side with, have caused us to, without knowing our fellow citizens, either hate them, or feel a primal urge to protect them as if they were a treasured ally?

At any rate, to get back on track, early in my bid at Bare Hill, a time when support from the people on "my team" was flowing in almost daily, one day I received a letter from a bright eyed and bushy tailed Marine Corps machine gunner named Alexander Oakes. Now what I found intriguing about this letter was that, unlike everybody else who had written to me, the author of this letter proudly declared himself to not be on my side of the political aisle. Rather, he was just a sane citizen who had seen my case, analyzed the evidence, and decided that, regardless of our political differences, the case against me was not only utterly weak and/or politically motivated, but also that the justification for my actions (self-defense) were clearly evident. In other words, the perversion of the law for political ends disgusted him, and because of this he felt that the least he could do is share some kind words, express his support, and send some short stories to help me pass the time.

These initial attempts to brighten my day, put frankly, succeeded. More than that, though, they eventually led to a full blown friendship. This is to say that while I was in Bare Hill, we ended up writing letters to each other that were so lengthy that we would have to classify them as packages. In fact, at one point these letters got so dense that I began having to trade cigarettes and fish steaks for extra stamps.

Anyway, during these discourses, whenever we discussed political issues he would always offer a perspective that I didn't see, and even more beneficial, at least to me, he would also point out when my sense of morality, my values, my views on the constitution, and/or my partisanship would contradict one another. Furthermore, when discussing international politics he would offer real world experience that I didn't have since he was a veteran of a foreign war, even when that perspective was inconvenient, and not really what I "wanted" to hear. Oh yeah, and as a bonus he was also in college studying politics at this time, which meant that he had simply learned and/or knew some things that I just didn't.

Alex and I continued writing each other for years after that initial letter, and when we wrote each other, each time he would tell me about his academic accomplishments, which are many, and include his writings, which, as time went on, evolved from fictional stories to academic essays, then to complex analyses, and finally to actual novels/articles. And all the while his genuine desire to make a positive difference on the country by enriching the thought processes of his fellow Americans became ever clearer.

Eventually, I was released from prison. When this occurred, I kept in touch with Alex and witnessed his continued hard work ethic as he toiled thanklessly to grow his podcast and publish articles, which was, to be honest, fun to watch. Anyway, when he completed *The Sane Citizens Political Handbook* and presented it for me to read, I found it to be his best work yet and felt honored that he would ask me to write the foreword for it.

You see, people can get so worked up over classifying the members of each political party as either good guys or bad guys, and I'm a witness to this and, unfortunately, even guilty of it myself on occasion. What I mean by this is that our evaluations of our "fellow man's" argument is often based purely on the messenger. I.e., when hearing the rebuttal to a stance one feels strongly about, more often than not people in the US will simply prepare a counterattack instead of actually hearing the message out. All based on whether there is an "R" or a "D" after the messenger's name.

Now in my experience the result of engaging in this type of "politicking" is that the citizens of this great country quite often find themselves proudly declaring their full support for an action that is, in all reality, in direct contradiction to their core values; and generally they are not even aware of it because they are blinded by tribe loyalty! Needless to say I think, like Alex, that this status quo is a travesty because the fact of the matter is that every American, regardless of who they voted for, needs to sometimes step back, put aside their partisan leanings, and analyze the big picture so that they can realize if they're being fooled into taking a foolish stance simply because it's being presented by one of "the good guys". And the reason for this is because, if they don't, well, they may find themselves happy to discard their constitutional rights for short-term political gains, and/or imprison a person whom they've never met and know nothing about, simply because of that aforementioned tribe loyalty.

In closing, sometimes the other party across from you at the ballot box has genuine concerns and/or good ideas that are worth considering. Furthermore, there is no future in a country where the partisan divide is so deep that honest discussions cannot be had without insults and/or violence. This is why Alex writing this book is so important, and not only to Americans I might add, but also to passionate partisan actors who love liberty across the globe. This is to say that his ability to analyze political conflict in a non-partisan manner is needed now more than ever; especially in a world where, thanks to invention of social media, the ability to to attack those who disagree with you has never been easier. In any case, this book is guaranteed to offer you an analysis of politics that you'll never hear from your favorite political pundits, who, at the end of the day, are generally just slaves to their party. In other words, in *The Sane Citizens Political Handbook* Alex cuts through the muddy waters of political talking points to present the unbiased and non-partisan truth that, in my experience, every American craves. So, get comfortable, grab a beer or your favorite snack, and put on your thinking cap, because once you do sit down with this book, which I am confident you'll find as addicting as I did, you won't want to get back up until it's done. Enjoy.

Introduction

Politics. Even though I am a politics junkie, in today's landscape this word rings bittersweet in my ears. On one hand, I believe that politics, the divisions that come with them, and the power structures they form have the potential to destroy, not just human life, but all life on planet Earth. On the other hand, however, I believe that politics, their ability to allow us to ideologically organize with like-minded people, and their usefulness in solving large-scale societal problems make them perhaps the greatest tool we as humans have when it comes to fostering the advancement, in all ways, of our species. Of course, people will say that this is just me blowing the importance of politics out of proportion, and I do get that. I mean, after all it makes sense that someone who has dedicated their life to studying, analyzing, and publicly commentating on politics would take it a bit more seriously than the average Joe who just wants to earn a paycheck, raise a family, and take their boat out on the lake for the weekend. With that said, though, I think that this broadly held mindset of passive political observation is a great travesty and one that actually runs counter to what this great nation is all about. Let me explain.

Aristotle, the Godfather of political science, once stated that *"Hence it is evident that the state is a creation of nature, and that man is by nature a political animal. And he who by nature and not by mere accident is without a state, is either above humanity, or below it; he is the 'Tribeless, lawless, hearthless one,' whom Homera denounces—the outcast who is a lover of war; he may be compared to a bird which flies alone."* If this statement is true, and my understanding of history and human sociology would suggest that it is, then politics is not just for the economic elites, the academics, and/or the professional analyst class. Rather, it is a fundamental part of our human nature and something that we here in the US, a democratic republic, should all be a part of. Well, unfortunately, in modern American society politics has instead been framed, by the supposed subject matter experts, as a complicated and far-off thing that the average person need not worry about and this has led to a growing class of what renowned political scientist Philip E. Converse would call "unsophisticated voters."

Now this term, unsophisticated voters, at first glance reinforces the idea that politics is only for the professionals and the elites; or at least that there is a large class of people in our society that have no business being involved in the affair (i.e., most of us are too unsophisticated to understand politics). However, this is not what Converse actually means when he refers to unsophisticated voters. For instance, imagine we are talking about swimming. Put frankly, I know next to nothing about professional swimming. Nonetheless, every four years I click on the television, go to whatever channel is showing the Olympics, and then passionately root for whomever is representing the United States. I complain when I think something is unfair, decry the entire institution as corrupt when there is a rule or policy that I do not understand, and even start to see the other swimmers as merely my team's opposition. Well, despite this passionate fandom, when it comes to professional swimming, I am unsophisticated. In other words, even though I am an avid follower of swimming, at the end of the day I am only vaguely familiar with the sport and have not really sought out enough information about it to have a truly valid opinion on its inner workings.

In essence, this is how Converse views the casual American voter. This is to say that like me with swimming, when it comes to politics the average American is very passionate about their beliefs, however, for the most part they have not truly taken the time to understand these beliefs. Rather, they have outsourced this task to the "experts" and/or leaders of their respective teams (Republicans, Democrats, Libertarians, etc.). Now the reason I say this is a travesty is because one of the things that makes America unique is that, unlike the organizations that control/host swimming competitions, American politics are open to anyone who is a United States citizen. In other words, whether you are a political professional or just a casual observer, at the end of the day, we all have an equal amount of influence when it comes time to vote.

Of course, this is a good thing and I would even go so far as to say that it is one of the main things that sets us apart, in a positive way, from most of the other countries that we share a planet with; but with that said, with this equality in representation, as with any power, comes responsibility, and this responsibility is one that unsophisticated voters are just not equipped to handle. Therefore, the existence of so many unsophisticated voters, or if you prefer "passive observers", is unfortunate because We the People of the United States of America, a country that has the most powerful military/economy in all of human history, were never supposed to take our ability to participate in politics for granted, and we were certainly never supposed to allow that power to be monopolized by only a few select voices.

Anyway, to avoid going into a full-on rant, let me just say that, in sum, American politics do in fact matter, and therefore, it is each and every one of our responsibility, nay, our constitutional duty to be an active and sophisticated participate in this nation's politics because what makes this country unique and special, according to my analyses, is very simple. It is not that we are a Christian nation, it is not that we promote liberal values and/or equality, and it is not that we have this amendment or that one. No, what makes this country so special is that our country, The United States of America, constitutionally recognizes and enshrines the power of We the People over the nation-state and this means that we are not subjects of a king, loyalists of a monarchy, or slaves to an authoritarian dictator; rather it means that we are citizens who consent to be governed, and as citizens who consent to be governed the founders of this great nation, whatever you may think about them as individuals, have charged us, the people, with the tasks of guiding American politics, and also holding to account those who go against that constitutional power structure.

Alright, now that you know what my views are about having an active US citizenry, I want to move on to my goals for this book. In essence, my two main goals in this book are to provide the politically "unsophisticated" with an easy-to-understand overview of a few of the most divisive issues in US politics and for us, together, to find a sane position on these issues. Now because I want to remain as objective as possible during this journey, in lieu of using one of the two main political ideologies (conservative/liberal) as a foundation for my sanity, which most political books would do, I will instead be using the United States Constitution to conduct a quality check of each and every position we arrive at. The reason for this is that in our day and age US politics has, for the unsophisticated and sophisticated alike, moved away from the guidance of our founding documents and instead to a political Colosseum wherein everything revolves around one team beating the other team (i.e., Republicans vs. Democrats). Well, at least that is how I see it. At any rate, as you will come to find out during this book, I despise both of the major political parties in the United States and see them both as entities working for their own personal agendas, not We the People. Ergo, instead of using them as my North Star I will be using the US Constitution, even if it isn't quite as sexy.

Now on the topic of our founding documents there is something I need to address right off the bat. Look, I get it. Some of you may not like the Constitution, and hell, you may be right. But nonetheless, for right now the United States Constitution is what we have, and it is quite literally what this entire nation is founded on. So, whether you are like me, someone who thinks that the US Constitution is the best one of its kind ever to be created (flaws and all), or you are someone who believes the United States Constitution is a bad document (or at least one that we should alter), it doesn't change the fact that if you are an American citizen the US Constitution is the legal and technical gold standard by which this country should be run. Therefore, like it or not, using this document as the final quality check for my various sane positions is undeniably the most logical thing to do if I wish to remain unbiased toward any one side of the aisle over the other.

Moving on, as I suggested a couple of paragraphs ago, the political landscape of this country, in my view, and probably yours if you picked up this book, has turned into little more than a sports game wherein each side cares only about beating the other side, not about what is actually right and/or constitutional. As a result, when I observe these conflicts between the two sides, I often notice quite a bit of a disconnect. This is to say that much like two ships, one occupied by donkeys and the other by elephants, missing each other in the night (while also shooting cannons wildly into the air at one another I might add), when members of the two parties interact/debate, they all too often miss the other sides point entirely. I.e., the abortion debate, for instance, generally devolves into one side screaming about how the other side wants to remove women's rights while the other side screams about how that side wants to kill babies instead of both sides realizing that what they are actually arguing about is where does life begin. Now I cannot say whether or not this type of political participation is the design of a powerful and nefarious force, though I have my suspicions that is, but I can say with some certainty that it seems unnecessarily divisive, and therefore is something I want to remedy.

Now, the way I will be approaching this task, remedying this unnecessary divide, that is, is by using what Dr. Owen Anderson refers to as a reverse Hegelian Dialectic. Of course, I know that many of you will not be familiar with this concept, so let me explain what I mean by reverse Hegelian Dialectic first before moving on.

SIDENOTE

In the academic community, and more specifically the field of philosophy, there are a lot of different views on what a regular Hegelian Dialectic actually is. This is not a book explicitly about philosophy and therefore I will not be going through all of these positions. I simply want to explain what a Hegelian Dialectic is as I have come to understand it, what a reverse Hegelian Dialectic is, again, as I have come to understand it, and also how I plan to use these tools of thought to find sane positions.

First described by Enlightenment German philosopher Georg Wilhelm Friedrich Hegel, the Hegelian Dialectic is a mechanism used to arrive at a final truth or conclusion and Hegel explained this as a process wherein truth is derived through the friction and conflict between one force and its opposite. In other words, a Hegelian Dialectic is where two competing ideas, a thesis and an anti-thesis, clash until they form a new position, the synthesis, which according to Hegel is a better solution. Then, this new conclusion, which took the best of the prior positions and combined them, will become a new thesis, thus causing a new antithesis to form that opposes it. Then, as you may have guessed, that ensuing conflict will lead to yet another synthesis, and so on and so forth. Then, in theory, this process will repeat over and over again until a final synthesis is revealed, which, theoretically, is absolute truth. In lay terms, the Hegelian Dialectic is a battle between two extreme positions that will eventually lead to a result that is somewhere in the middle. Then, that middle position will develop an opposing position of its own and after they battle a new result, in the middle of those two positions, will form, thus moving us closer to the "best" conclusion. Make sense?

As you can see the Hegelian Dialectic has a lot of potential when it comes to refining/improving ideas, however, despite its usefulness in philosophy, when it comes to politics I actually believe that the opposite approach is what we need. To explain, during one of his most impactful lectures about the Hegelian Dialectic, the aforementioned Dr. Anderson stated, "In terms of ultimate truth, would it not be more beneficial to apply a somewhat opposite approach? A reverse Hegelian Dialectic if you will." Now this statement, at the time, did not seem that significant to me. After all, I was still completing my undergrad and was only taking his course about religion and philosophy in order to fulfill one of my elective requirements. But be that as it may, as I moved into graduate school, wherein independent political research became a much more significant part of my curriculum, it finally hit me that a reverse Hegelian Dialectic could be the exact tool we need to remedy some of our country's ideological divisions, which as I mentioned before, I deem to be largely unnecessary.

You see, the issue with the original Hegelian Dialectic, at least in terms of politics, is that it, by design, forces the fringes of ideological thought against one another, and if you look though human history, particularly postmodern human history, this has, in my opinion, resulted in some less-than-ideal final outcomes. Here are just a few examples of this:

> **Thesis:** *British and French power hegemony after World War 1*
> **Anti-thesis:** *Hitler*
> **Synthesis:** *USA hegemony (endless wars, international conflicts over sovereignty, attempts by China to destabilize the US dollar, etc.)*

> **Thesis:** *Traditional conservatism*
> **Anti-thesis:** *Marxism*
> **Synthesis:** *Globalism (Loss of American Self-Identity and pride, large scale/inefficient international bureaucracies, unipolar vs a bipolar world, etc.)*

> **Thesis:** *US government losing domestic power*
> **Anti-thesis:** *9/11*
> **Synthesis:** *Patriot Act, NSA spying*

> **Thesis:** *Feminism*

Anti-thesis: *PUA (pick-up artist), MRA (men's right's activist's),*
neo masculinity

Synthesis: *Gender Theory*

Of course, perhaps in a thousand years it will become clear that all of these syntheses have been a net positive for humanity, but at this point, it seems to me that each of these syntheses has resulted in, or at least exasperated the largescale ideological divisions that exist within our species and this is especially true in the Western world, and more specifically the United States. Case in point, whether we are looking at discretionary spending, foreign policy, or how to help underperforming communities, from my viewpoint, and likely yours, the US is more ideologically divided than ever. Now I know this language may make you roll your eyes because you have heard it so often alongside fearmongering reports of impending civil war and a potential national divorce, but the truth is that the ideological fracturing we have seen in our country over the last 15 or so years is actually much more serious than any revolution and/or civil war style conflict that may or may not happen.

This is because, unlike kids on a playground who have it out in a physically violent conflict only to become friends later on because, after all, they are part of the same school, same class, and same in/group; our civilization is under the false assumption that we are, at a foundational level, members of many different in/groups (i.e., Republican, Democrat, POC, Gender Queer, Conservative, Social Liberal, etc.), all of which end up being boiled down into one of two political ideologies that are nothing alike. Ergo, where the kids on the playground will wipe the blood from their noses and become friends, or at the very least become civil enough through mutual respect to stay the hell out of each other's way and coexist, the US population has chosen to not even confront the other side as humans, much less fellow American's. In other words, we have tossed one another aside as garbage for the sin of disagreeing because, through our lazy deductive reasoning, we have established ourselves as morally superior to all those who have different beliefs than us, and when we do this, divide everyone in the population into either a friend or foe based on their personal politics that is, we set a dangerous precedent of making our fellow Americans either good or evil; even though we are all technically still part of the same in/group, United States citizens living under the guidance and direction of the US Constitution. I.e., if my fellow man is in opposition to myself then he is not, in fact, my fellow man, but rather the antithesis to morality and therefore my enemy. Get it?

Anyway, when it comes to solving this division you may be wondering where a reverse Hegelian Dialectic fits in. Well, put plainly, instead of pitting the prominent political ideologies against one another until I find a new conclusion for each issue, what I want to do in this book is to take some of the most controversial ideological issues in American politics and investigate them until I actually get back to the *original* point of disagreement. In other words, instead of finding new more advanced answers to our political strife, I want to trace things back to where the two major American political ideologies actually disagreed in the first place.

Now the logic behind using this reverse Hegelian Dialectic is that it should allow me, and you as well, to better understand the root of our national disagreements. This is to say that instead of trying to move farther away from any two positions in an attempt to find an altogether new starting point; I seek to study the debates surrounding the issues in this book in order to refine a synthesis that draws on the strengths of both sides, with the goal being to find a sane and reasonable position. And my hope is that by doing this, finding the point for each issue in which the left and right sides of the aisle split ways that is, is that I can establish a new, constitutionally grounded position that we can all at least somewhat agree on. Ergo, when it is all said and done, this book that is, I hope that this work actually helps us move forward as a nation toward more prosperous and sensible ideological positions. Positions, I might add, that We the People can force our elected leaders to respect and listen to through the imposing of our constitutionally established political power and influence. So, that is where the reverse Hegelian Dialectic fits in. Basically, it will allow us to figure out where both sides went crazy.

Alright, moving on, now that you know what my goals are for this book, as well as how I aim to accomplish them, I need to address just two things before moving on to the first issue. First off, most of us these days, me included, have short attention spans. Because of this, I have tried to avoid getting too long-winded whilst analyzing the various issues I bring up in this book. As a result, you may notice that some of the chapters are very short, only a couple of pages, while others are more complex ones and, in some cases, rather long. So, just know that my desire to get all of this information out there succinctly is the reason that the chapter lengths vary so much and try not to let it bother you. Furthermore, if you do find that some of the chapters are not long enough for your taste, well, then I would advise you go through the references section for those chapters and use those resources to conduct your own follow-on research. Good to go?

Second, I am not going to delve too far into race relations and gender equality in this book, even though they will come up from time to time. The reason for this is simple. You see, the constitutional position on these topics is that all people are created equal and should be afforded equal rights. Now as a country we have not always lived up to that, but in our current day and age, people are so against those past mistakes that they are actually trying to go the other direction in an attempt to get revenge for those past injustices. So, put plainly, those who discriminated against others in the past based on race and gender were wrong, and people discriminating against groups today in order to make up for that past are also wrong. In other words, the sane position on these issues is rather self-evident. Don't judge people and/or treat them better or worse than any other group of people based on their immutable characteristics. Got it?

SIDENOTE

If you disagree with that position on race and gender and you instead think that certain groups are lesser and/or deserve fewer rights; or that certain groups deserve special treatment to counteract the beliefs of those people, then your position is counter to the equality spoken of in our Constitution and your position, in my view, is quite flawed. Ergo, if you are for any type of race/gender based discrimination, even discrimination against white people, your position is, put frankly, insane. Capeesh? Sweet, then moving forward let that be all there is to say on that topic.

Well folks, that is the end of this introduction. In closing, I want to be clear that I do not want this book to turn into a tool for any particular side of the partisan spectrum to whack the other one with. In fact, my goal is for it to help us get past the partisanship hackery I see in most publicized political debates altogether because

I truly believe that if we are to improve the political landscape of the United States, which is supposed to be the beacon for individual liberty that shines across the world, we, as an active citizenry, must find some unity and/or specific points of agreement that are rooted in something stronger than a political team and/or political identity. So, no. I do not want people to cherry pick chapters so that they can "beat" the other side while ignoring the rest of the book. Instead, I hope that this book simply helps We the People of the United States of America find more sane and constitutional ways to pull the levers of American political power. Alright, with all of that said, let's begin.

CHAPTER 2

Partisanship

A cheap glass bottle full of gasoline soars through the crisp evening air and explodes as it connects with the wet Seattle asphalt showering a line of police officers with the acrid stench of burning fuel. A bullet sent into motion by the trigger pull of a 15-year-old American farmer wearing a tattered grey uniform whirs through the air until it embeds itself in the neck of a Union soldier. A black man in 1952 is arrested and beaten by a county Sheriff for going into a white business. Then, in that same location seventy years later a white woman is beaten mercilessly by black teens and called a chalk monkey. All the while the economic and political elites sit upon their thrones and watch us peasants toil before them, divided.

As history has shown us, the United States is no stranger to ideological division and for most of our tenure, a plurality of us have been obsessed with our racial, religious, and/or political identities. We have abused one another, outright denied each other's humanity, and in some cases, we have even ended up slaying one another; and if I'm being honest, sometimes it feels like not much has changed. This is to say that despite decades of successfully undoing divisive policies and eradicating discriminatory cultural norms, as you may have noticed, we are still experiencing a significant amount of inter-group division within our country. Well, a major source of this division, and what this chapter specifically addresses, is the stark divide between our two major political parties, both of which currently represent one side of the infamous left-right continuum.

In my summation, the recent increase in temperature regarding the left vs right divide among the American populace is likely due to either the widespread availability of political information brought forth by the internet revolution, the modern-day infusion of politics into culture, or both. Now we could spend a whole chapter arguing my position on this, but that would be, essentially, a waste of our time because regardless of what the underlying cause actually is, as of right now this rift between the Republican and Democrat parties seems like it is here to stay. And just to make matters worse, this left vs right divide now seems to have permeated much deeper than the Oval Office and/or the halls of Congress. In other words, within the borders of modern-day America, the debate between the political left and the political right appears to have become an integral part of every single facet of modern life. This is to say that no longer are we living in the days wherein your partisan alignment was a private and personal part of who you are that, in reality, only mattered on election day. Instead, now we live in a world in which what political party you side with determines who you can be friends with, what movies you can watch, what music you can listen to, and even what beer you are allowed to drink. Make the wrong decision in any of these areas and you are cast out of your tribe and left to either traverse the cold and merciless political landscape alone, or more likely turncoat and join the opposing side. So, in America why do people on the right (Republicans/Conservatives) and people on the left (Democrats/ Liberals) hate each other so much, and is this degree of division what the founding fathers envisioned? Well, in order to answer this let's first start by taking a look at how our biology factors in, shall we?

SIDENOTE

The term "other" has been hijacked by groups on the fringes of the left side of the left/right continuum, but I do not use this term in the way they do. In other words, when I say the "other" I am simply referring to in-group/out-group dynamics, which are a well-established aspect of human behavior. So, don't get confused when you hear me use this term and/or misinterpret it.

— ALSO —

Moving forward you should know that an in-group refers to an exclusive group of people with a shared interest and/or identity, and an out-group refers to any group of people that do not belong to that in-group.

From an evolutionary perspective, I would argue that there are many reasons to dislike one another in a world as big and connected as the one we currently reside in. In fact, when it comes to our fellow Americans, I would be willing to wager that there is actually more to dislike about one another than there is to like. If you were keeping a tally anyway. At any rate, this stems from basic in-group/out-group theory, which is a concept that is closely tied to something called a biological immune system. In essence, the biological immune system is an evolutionarily developed part of who we are as humans and broadly speaking it serves the purpose of making us highly resistant to and/or cautious of anyone who is different.

SIDENOTE

At face value this part of our biology sounds bad, but the reality is that this tendency to dislike/distrust the "other" is actually quite important and has been one of the main aspects of our nature helping to keep our kind safe and secure for tens of thousands of years. In other words, this natural instinct of being cautious and distrustful of outsiders probably helped your ancestors keep from getting their heads bashed in while they slept by the drifter staying in their guest cave.

Now despite how this aspect of our biology looks on the surface, after doing my own research on human behavior, I do have to say that, at the very least, this natural distrust of the outsider is not only "not inherently bad", but actually rather important because without it the human species quite likely would not exist. You see, it doesn't take a rocket scientist to know that humans survive best in groups, right? Well, according to the social sciences establishing a common enemy often acts as a catalyst that bonds human groups together and turns them into tight-knit communities that handle outside threats exceptionally well. In other words, whether your camp is being attacked by a saber tooth tiger or your buildings are having planes smashed into them, adversity brought on by an outside threat almost always leads to in-group unification, which has been and still is necessary if human societies plan to flourish in the face of struggle. So, yes, there is some utility to this biological immmune system in that it fosters the creation of stable in-groups.

Of course, as with any pattern of human behavior, this benefit does also go the other way. To clarify, in some situations wherein no external threat large enough to truly threaten the in-group exists, natural friction from within the group generally occurs and can actually drive that group apart and pit those in it against one another; and I suppose that you can blame this habit of ours, in part, on the fact that at the end of the day we are still designed, in a way, to find an enemy for our in-group to rally against, even if that means "breaking up" the current in-group. I digress though. This biological tendency of needing to have an enemy, in essence, is what has happened to the United States. In other words, we have the largest and most powerful in-group to ever exist in all of human history, so, if we are to find an enemy, it will likely have to come from within. Of course, there are still rare occurrences wherein an outside threat does temporarily unite us, such as 9/11, for instance, but for the most part we here in America, a country surrounded by oceans on two sides and non-threatening militaries on the other two, have nothing else to focus our natural instincts on other than our fellow Americans.

SIDENOTE

To add to this conundrum, our habit of making an enemy from within only becomes easier to embrace when our nation is so neatly, or so it appears, divided into two discernable boxes. This is to say that when the entire country has been divided into "left-wingers" and "right-wingers," essentially, all the work of finding an in-group enemy has already been done for you. Ergo, all you have to do is pick a side.

Alright, now that you know a little bit about why it is so easy, and also natural for us to make enemies (I wish I had more time to spend on this, but if you want more information look through the references!), I think that we should end our biology discussion and instead move into where the terms right and left first came from and how they/should not should be applied today. The reason for this is because, as it stands now, these are currently the two main in-groups in the United States, politically speaking that is, and therefore the divide between these in-groups is where a lot of our *overall* division stems from. Sound like a plan? Great, let's get into it.

So our discussion about the origins of the terms left and right begins in 18th-century France because during this period France underwent some significant political changes that actually ended up leading to the birth of these two terms. Now to give you an overview of these changes, France up until this time had been under the control of what was known as the Ancien Régime, or Old Regime. This was, essentially, a feudal system similar to what we saw in medieval times. In other words, in feudal systems the king would allow certain nobles and high-status individuals to operate their own personal estates, but in the end, he still theoretically owned everything within his kingdom. Furthermore, in these feudal systems there generally existed a large class of serfs and peasants, who in France's case, made up roughly 98% of the population, and to put it lightly, these individuals typically did not have many rights and basically just existed to serve the king and his nobles. Well, partially due to the accessibility of pro-revolution literature, and partially due to economic hardships brought on by the French crown's participation in the American Revolution, when it came to France in the late 18th century the Ancien Régime became very unpopular among this 98% of the population. As a result, in 1789 the Old Regime was removed, and in its place the National Constituent Assembly was formed. Now unlike the Old Regime, this new assembly was extremely popular among that 98%, in part, because it made many changes to the country's political practices in support of the "common man." For instance, one of the assembly's first moves was to implement something called the *Declaration of the Rights of Man and of the Citizen*, which, among other things, sought to elevate liberty, equality, the inviolability of property, and the right to resist oppression.

Anyway, even though this new style of government was quickly accepted, especially so by the lower classes, it was still a highly unstable system because the former ruling class, as one would expect, did not like the idea of giving up their power. Ergo, it didn't take long until this instability was intentionally exasperated these old rulers and as a result this instability eventually culminated into the National Constituent Assembly fracturing into two distinct factions. The first, which was a group of anti-royalist revolutionaries who opposed the existence of a feudal-style monarchy, were comprised of members of the middle-class Third Estate, which was a political entity that had previously had only one-third of the political power in the country despite making up most of its inhabitants, and this faction, who sat on the left side of the assembly when it was in session, opposed the Old Regime and instead wanted a new republic style of government that gave equal rights and political power to all of the members of the country, not just the wealthy elites. Thus, they were called leftists.

Now on the other side of the literal and proverbial aisle, however, the second faction, which consisted of the aristocrats, the clergymen, and the nobles, opposed these leftists and instead supported the idea of keeping things as they were. This is to say that they wished to maintain the power of the monarchy, as the country had done in the past, and leave the "common man," for the most part, out of politics. Ergo, since they were not leftists, they ended up congregating on the right side of the assembly, when it was in session that is, thus making this faction quite literally the party of the right. Pretty crazy, right…ok, bad pun. At any rate, that is where the terms left and right actually come from.

Ok, now that we know where these two terms come from, let's talk about how we can use these terms in the context of today's political landscape. So, the terms left and right, in politics, come from the physical seating locations of the French National Constituent Assembly's two factions. Furthermore, when it comes to the actual ideological differences between these two factions, in essence, their main disagreement was whether or not they should relinquish King Louis XVI's power in order to install a new more liberal/progressive version of government or whether or not they should conserve the more traditional and long-standing form of government that gave a significant amount of power to that same king. Good to go? Well, since we want to apply this left/right continuum to US politics, it will be easier to think of the left vs right divide, from this point forward, simply as a change vs no change divide. In other words, the left side of the aisle represents the side of change, and the right side of the aisle represents the side of maintaining the current status quo.

SIDENOTE

If it is easier for you, simply think about left and right in terms of liberal and conservative with liberal being the term that refers to change, and conservative being the word that refers to no change. If you decide to think in these terms, though, just do not make the mistake of correlating these terms with Republican and Democrat. Now the reason for this will become clearer as we move forward, but in essence, liberal and conservative are specific terms that represent specific ideologies, not political parties, which as you will see shortly have a tendency to change their ideological stances rather often and are thus not good examples of specific belief systems.

Alright, now that you know not only where the terms left and right come from, but also how to use them in today's political landscape, let's analyze if these terms still accurately reflect the two main factions running our politics here in the US. In other words, let's take a look into our own country's past and figure out where the Republican and Democrat parties actually came from and what they stand for today since, after all, these two parties are the current flag bearers of these ideologies (left/liberal; right/conservative), and therefore are a critical piece of this left/right puzzle. To begin, let's go all the way back to the beginning, shall we?

As most of you reading and/or listening to this know, the United States of America was birthed into existence in 1776, and this new nation, which was the first of its kind, was founded on individual liberty. Sure, before the United States of America, societies like those of the Greeks had created various forms of democracy that were admittedly revolutionary for their time, but the key difference in the founding documents of this country was that unlike the Greeks, whose state merely recognized the people's right to participate in government, embedded in our Constitution is the inherent ownership of the government by its citizens. Now this constitutional recognition of the people's power over the government is what, in my view, separates the United States of America from its counterparts and is one of the main aspects of our country that make it great; but with that said, one of the negative outcomes of this "government for the people by the people" is that it has made the two major political parties, essentially, anyone's dog for a bone. This is to say that in a system wherein the wills and desires of We the People control who gets elected, quite often the people who want to win those elections will tell us whatever we want to hear, thus making them a faction without a sturdy foundation, as well as a faction open to largescale and unpredictable change. With that in mind, let's go through the history of America's political factions so that you can see what I am talking about for yourself.

As fate would have it, in the first days of this country, technically, there were no formal political parties, however, it did not take long until this changed and, much like the National Constituent Assembly during the French Revolution, the political elites started to form organized and identifiable factions. The first of these American factions was the Federalist faction, and its main supporters were people like George Washington, Alexander Hamilton, and John Jay. Now when it came to the ideology of the Federalists, in essence, they supported a strong central government and all of the things, like a central bank, that came with it. Ergo, if it makes it easier, you can think of this as the "big government" party of 18th century America.

In stark opposition to these Federalists, on the other hand, was a faction led by Thomas Jefferson, James Madison, and James Monroe, and this faction, among other things, strongly opposed a centralized government and was instead in favor of a lion's share of the government's power being given to the individual states. Ergo, they were, for all intents and purposes, the party of the people and/or small government, and as a result got the nickname of "Anti-Federalists." Of course, the name Anti-Federalists was a little on the nose as far as names went, so they quickly opted to change the name, and henceforth became known officially as the Democrat-Republicans.

Now, at this point in the early days of American history, given what we know about the origins of the terms left and right, the Federalists could be described as being on the left and the Democrat-Republicans on the right. This is because the Federalists were in favor of a government that more closely resembled Britain's government, a government that had a significant amount of centralized power, and the Democrat-Republicans wanted a more decentralized government, which, technically speaking, adhered closer our "liberty-loving" Constitution. Furthermore, I suppose that, given the importance our founding documents place on individual liberty, at this point in time the Federalists were also technically liberals and the Democrat-Republicans were technically conservatives. This is because the Federalists wanted to change the status quo of government away from the Constitution's mandate for individual liberty, while the Democrat-Republicans actually wanted to adhere closer to this Constitution, or in other words, conserve the status quo of a decentralized system.

Now I know that all of these terms and/or classifications can bend the mind a bit, but as mentioned in the margin sidenote above, left, or liberal, simply refers to change, and right, or conservative, simply refers to no change. So, since the status quo of the United States is the US Constitution, and this document is founded on individual liberty, any move away from individual liberty, regardless of what party is currently in power, would be a move in favor of change. Therefore, as long as you remember that basic aspect of the left/right divide, what I just said about these two parties should make sense? Anyway, let's move on to the next significant change in the history of America's political parties.

Despite both of these parties gaining a significant amount of power in those early days, eventually, following the War of 1812, the

Federalist faction dissolved leaving only the Democrat-Republican party. This did not mean an end to the left-right division in US politics, though, and after a close presidential election in 1824 between Andrew Jackson and John Quincy Adams the Democrat-Republican party underwent a split. I.e., the Democrat-Republicans, who would shortly thereafter simply become the Democrats, a title that obviously remains in use to this day, stayed put while John Quincy Adams and Henry Clay broke off and founded the Whig Party, and this new party, which would eventually become the Republican party in 1854 after it was rebirthed with the goal of ending slavery, existed from the 1830s until the Civil War. But at any rate the main disagreement between these two parties was, once again, centered around the size and scope of the federal government. In other words, much like the National Constituent Assembly during the French Revolution, these two factions could not find common ground when it came to the problem of allocating political power.

Now as far as who was left and who was right when it came to these parties, because the Democrats were in favor of a smaller Federal government and against a central bank, during this time period they would technically be considered on the right. The Whig party, on the other hand, was quite open about its support of a central bank, increased tariffs, and Federal financial aid being distributed in response to several financial crises, so, it is reasonable to say that they were closer to the left side of the political spectrum during this time, even though, as I said before, they are the party that would eventually become the Republicans, who, as it stands now, are known as the right-wingers. Confusing, I know. Anyway, to put a bow on this pre-20th century period, given that this country was founded on individual liberty, not large and/or overarching federal bodies of centralized control, it would appear that from the late 18th century until the civil war the Democrats were actually the right-wingers and the Whig/Republican party the left-wingers. Of course, this very clearly isn't the case today, so, what changed?

Well, as fate would have it there was not one single event, per se, that caused these parties to swap sides on the left-right continuum, which again, is simply a change vs no change continuum (With the change referring to changing our constitutional framework). Rather, from the 1860s to 1936 there were actually many changes that fostered this switch. For instance, during this aforementioned period there was a new widespread and bipartisan concern for social justice among the American population that had not been seen before. You see, the American Civil War was about a lot of different things, however, it would be somewhat difficult to argue against the idea that slavery was a major part of why this war happened. I mean, as I mentioned earlier, this issue was quite literally the reason for the birth of Lincoln's Republican party. Anyway, during this 1860s-1936 period a heightened concern about matters of social justice and equality among the electorate, the group to whom our Constitution grants the majority of America's political power, drove the political elites to place more focus on these issues than they had previously. In particular, a notable and influential Democrat by the name of William Jennings Bryan, who was well-known for negotiating several important peace treaties following the end of World War I, muddied the partisan waters and blurred the lines between Republicans and Democrats in the eyes of the voters by pushing the Democrat party to expand Federal power in order to promote social justice objectives, which had traditionally been the stance of the Whig party, and then later on the Republican party.

Now as this social justice change was going on in the East, changes in the American West were occurring as well. You see, the westward expansion was creating a vibrant new voting bloc and opening up a massive, previously unavailable new area full of economic potential that big businesses could use to make money. In light of this plethora of new money-making opportunities, the Republicans, who had historically been the party of the wealthy, and therefore favorable toward big government, saw the West as a place where a smaller government would actually be more beneficial because this would leave most of the infrastructure building, like the Transcontinental Railroad, for instance, to the private sector. Ergo, even though this small government stance was new for the party, since it aligned with its financial needs at the time it was quickly accepted, and subsequently became a major part of their political platform. Now the Democrats, however, saw a different opportunity in the American West. This is to say that instead of business opportunities, they saw a budding opportunity to increase their political power by attracting new voters. In essence, their mindset was that they could sway these new voters to support their political ambitions by implementing Federally funded social welfare programs that promised to help the "little guy" instead of the large corporations, which was a move that received a lot of support from people like the small-time farmers who had also decided to go West.

At any rate, all of these things happening in concert with one another began to blur the lines between the two parties, and this blurring of the lines came to a peak in 1936 when Franklin D. Roosevelt was reelected as President of the United States; which happened, according to most historians, in large part due to the popularity of Roosevelt's New Deal, which was essentially a collection of government-funded programs designed to help the populace recover after the Great Depression. Regardless of the reason, though, by the time our country reached 1936 and Roosevelt was securely seated in the Oval office, the lines were no longer blurred and when the portrait of our political landscape came into focus the Democrats had fully made the transition to the party of big government, likely to garner the vote of the less-wealthy classes, and the Republicans had changed to the side of small government, likely in order to help their business interests. Well, that and because they had a deep dislike of President Roosevelt and wanted to oppose his administration at all costs, which was actually quite similar to the Whig party's creation around the shared goal of opposing Andrew Jackson's administration. Interesting how history sometimes doesn't take long to repeat itself, right? Anyway…

This new ideological organization of the parties has been and still is, at least officially, the status quo for each party. This is to say that the Republican Party, in theory, now stands for small government and more individual liberty, and the Democrat Party, in theory, now stands for a larger government that is focused, among other things, on fostering equality and social justice through centralized power. Now, since I decided to look at the left vs right continuum not as a spectrum of policy positions, but rather as a spectrum of change, with the liberal left being pro-change, and the conservative right being anti-change, given that the US Constitution is centered around the individual's power over the government and not the Federal government's power over us, this would make the small-government side the status quo side. Ergo, the Republican party, in theory, is now on the right side of the aisle, while the Democrat party, in theory, occupies the left.

Ok, so that is a quick down-and-dirty of where the terms left and right come from, as well as how they relate to the two major political parties active in the US today. Before moving on, though, I feel that I need to address something that pertains to the phrasing I used in that last paragraph. This is because I think you may be wondering why I kept emphasizing "in theory" when discussing what each party stands for. Well, the reason behind my decision to do this will make more sense in a bit, but just so you aren't totally confused, according to my own personal analyses, I would say that neither the Republican nor the Democrat party currently represents the right side of the aisle. In other words, I believe that both parties, in a way, are on the liberal left, or pro-change side of the left/right continuum. Again, this will make more sense in a bit when I talk about where we are currently in the Hegelian Dialectic of US politics, but before we get to that I want to first discuss the two-party system as a whole and the reason we still continue to use it because this will help you understand why the left/right divide is so crucial for sane citizens to understand.

SIDENOTE

As we are about to discuss, it is inevitable that in a winner take all system two parties will always hold the majority of the power. Therefore, in order to keep *our* system balanced and/or conducive to liberty, we must have one right-wing party, and one left-wing party.

Alright, so after everything we have talked about so far you may be wondering why here in the US, a country that currently contains more than 334 million people, we only have two major parties at any one given time. In other words, why do we appear to be slaves to this dichotomous left/right continuum instead of just having a bunch of parties? Well, in political science there is a concept known as Duverger's law and we are in luck because we actually can use this law to answer that very question.

In essence, Duverger's law holds that single-ballot (one vote per citizen), plurality rule elections (the person with the most votes wins), structured within single-member districts (only one person represents each district) tend to favor a two-party system. Now, the fancy way of saying this, which you can find on Wikipedia, is that "Duverger's law draws on a model of causality from the electoral system to a party system. A proportional representation system creates electoral conditions that foster the development of many parties, whereas a plurality system marginalizes smaller political parties, generally resulting in a two-party system." Of course, by now you know that I am not a huge fan of fancy, so in lay terms, Duverger's law dictates that in a winner take all system, wherein whoever gets the most votes wins the election, the way we think about voting is unnatural and the result is the emergence of only two major parties. In other words, in a winner take all system, as we have here in the United States, there is a psychological factor at play within the electorate that influences how we look at elections and how we vote. Ergo, in this type of system we are not necessarily incentivized to vote for whom we want; rather, we are more than likely going to vote for a person who, yes, we may still like, but who also has the best chance of winning since voting for anyone else seems like it would be, essentially, throwing away our vote.

So, in sum, because our elections are a zero-sum game, and one candidate on each side of the aisle will always be more popular than all the rest, voters realistically have only two choices, the candidate representing the left, or the candidate representing the right, when it comes time to enter the ballot box. Therefore, leading up to an election candidates and voters alike, assuming this law is correct, will subsequently flock to one of the two most popular parties, in our case the Republican and Democrat parties, instead of wasting their time on a less popular third option who likely won't be elected anyway. Make sense?

SIDENOTE

Now, a key phrase in that last sentence was "assuming this law is correct." Put plainly, it is. In fact, Duverger's law has held true in the United States since the very beginning and this is evidenced by the prominence of the Federalists and anti-Federalist in the late 18th century, the Federalists and Democrat-Republicans in the late 18th century/early 19th century, The Jacksonian Democrats and Whigs in the mid-19th century, and the Republican and Democrat parties ever since. And in addition to this well-documented political history, the statistical irrelevance of all third-party candidates in our countries over 200 years of election history only adds to the pile of evidence in support of Duverger's law.

Ok, so now you know not only the history of the left/right continuum, but also how it applies to our current political landscape, how we got the two parties that run that landscape, and also why these two parties are the only "real" parties in that landscape. Moving on, it is worth noting that because of the discovery of Duverger's law, many political theorists and analysts have criticized our winner take all system as they feel it does not accurately reflect the true desires of the voters. In fact, many of these subject matter experts believe that we should transition to another system entirely, such as a proportional voting system or an approval voting system, and as time goes on, I am starting to think that this may not be such a crazy idea. Hell, even George Washington himself warned against the creation of two opposing political parties because he felt they "are likely in the course of time and things, to become potent engines, by which cunning, ambitious, and unprincipled men will be enabled to subvert the power of the people and to usurp for themselves the reins of government, destroying afterward the very engines which have lifted them to unjust dominion." Of course, with this said it is still unlikely that any of these systems will be implemented, but just to be thorough, I still want to briefly discuss what these two other types of systems entail just so that you, the sane citizen, are aware of them.

SIDENOTE

This may be somewhat of a tangent, discussing alternative voting systems that is, but the reason I wanted to is because, as you no doubt have realized, I am not a huge fan of America's left/right divide. Therefore, I want these in the back of your mind because they help reinforce the idea that this left/right divide, which has taken the form of a Democrat/Republican divide, is not necessarily the only way to do things. Good to go?

Alright, starting with the proportional voting system, this style of election system is basically where the percentage of votes for a given party directly translates into the seats that party holds in the country's ruling body, and in these systems, which are popular in many European Union countries, smaller parties are not forced out but instead are allowed to become legitimate political entities. Now in lieu of doing the whole "in other words" thing, let's instead use a thought experiment containing two pretend examples so that we can compare our *plurality* voting system with a proportional voting system because this will help us see how each one actually looks in practice.

Plurality Voting System (which is what we have in the US): In 2026 America will vote in that year's mid-term elections. Now many seats will be up for grabs during this election season, such as senate seats, for instance, but let's focus on the congressional seats for this thought experiment. Well, during this 2026 election cycle, in many districts across the country two people, one from each side of the left/right continuum (one Democrat and one Republican), will battle it out to see who stands atop the proverbial political pyramid that governs their specific congressional district. This is to say that whoever wins these races will gain control of the whole district in its entirety and will not have to share their power with the other side.

Proportional Voting System: In a proportional voting system, however, many different parties (how many are allowed to run depends on the country) will end up putting forth legitimate candidates, not just the two most popular ones. For this example, let's say that five parties are allowed to run for control over the district since this is generally the go-to number in the West. Well, in a proportional voting system all five of these parties, regardless of who is the most popular, would end up with a seat at the table when the election dust cleared. Of course, some seats still may end up being bigger than others due to the fact that the power of this seat (voting rights within the governing body) would depend upon how many people actually voted for that party, but either way, all five parties would hold at least some political power. I.e., if 25% of the population voted for Party A then Party A would end up controlling 25% of the available seats in the district, and if another party, let's say Party C, only got 5% of the total votes instead of 25%, then, you got it, they will end up with

5% of the seats. In other words, in a proportional voting system all of the people in the electorate would be proportionally represented. Ergo, in the US instead of Congress being 50% Republican and 50% Democrat, perhaps it would be 35% Republican, 35% Democrat, 15% Libertarian, 5% Green Party, and 10% Independent. Get it?

Moving on, the second type of alternative system I mentioned earlier, an approval voting system, is one that allows people to vote for multiple candidates in each election. Now we will forgo the though experiment on this his type of system because Americans are kind of already aware of this system, at least in some areas. This is to say that here in America this type of voting system has already been attempted in places like New York, except here in the US we simply call it ranked-choice voting. In other words, in an approval voting system voters actually get to select more than one candidate on their ballot, the catch being that they have to rank them. So, for instance, instead of having to choose between one of the two major parties (Republicans and Democrats), in this type of system a voter will have the option to vote cast their ideal vote and/or a couple of safe votes. I.e., in the case of the 2026 midterms, a voter may decide that they really like the Green Party candidate for their district, and therefore will put them down first. However, since they think that it is unlikely this candidate will win, they may also end up placing the Democrat candidate second; and then, of course, whomever they liked "next best" after that. Ergo, the voter was able to vote for their true number one choice, while also doing their part to ensure that, should that less-popular candidate lose, their choice of the popular candidates still has a chance of winning, thus allowing them to vote how they want without "throwing away" their voting power. Make sense?

Now I think that this system is very interesting and is one that could do wonders for breaking up the stranglehold the Republicans and Democrats have over our political process, but with that said, unfortunately, this system still has some major flaws similar to our own. This is to say that, basically, approval voting systems still heavily favor a two-party system because, at the end of the day, it is still a winner take all system. So, more often than not, one of the two most popular and well-funded candidates will still win because they will still end up with a plurality of the votes. Anyway, that is enough about alternative systems that, in all likelihood, will never be implemented.

Ok, continuing ever onward toward our search for a sane position on partisanship, regardless of how healthy a winner takes all system is, put plainly, it's what we have to work with. But even though this is the case, and we live in, essentially, a political duopoly, I do want to stress that We the People are all still on the same team, even if we aren't. In other words, yes, at the end of the day we are all US citizens, and therefore on the American team, but more importantly, in a two-party system each side, if things are working correctly, should balance the other out. This is to say that if we live in a system of two parties, and these parties are constantly in opposition to one another, then this creates somewhat of a barrier to any one party having all of the power. So, even though we may disagree with one another over politics, if the goal is to remain free, well, then that means that Republicans need Democrats, and Democrats need Republicans, and therefore we shouldn't "hate" one another and/or see each other as political enemies. Let me explain.

Another way of looking at this is that if one side was to go away, or even lose a significant deal of power, we would essentially just end up living in a Monarchy controlled by one centralized faction that had no opposition. Ergo, yes, the next time you go to a ballot box in the US you will more than likely have a choice between only two realistic candidates, but during the other 729 days in between elections I feel that a reasonable and sane citizen should not be intellectually enslaved by a blind allegiance to this binary. This is to say that, outside of election day, the sane position is to look at both sides of the left/right continuum with an open mind, understand what they are disagreeing about (more than likely the role of the Federal Government in a specific issue), determine what the positive and negative aspects of both are, and then use that to guide what political actions you support while also realizing that the side opposite you helps to create balance in our system, and therefore is not compromised of people who are evil, but rather of American citizens who simply disagree with you about how to best wield the power of government and/or whether or not we should adjust our Constitutional status quo. I.e., on election day you may hate the other side, but in reality, you actually need there to be another side to ensure that our winner take all system is not controlled by only one faction, which, as history has shown us, does not work out very well.... looking at you Communists.

SIDENOTE

Just to reiterate, liberal and conservative technically refer to, in lay terms, change, and no change. This is an important classification to make at the beginning of this book because the two major parties and their pundits have regularly hijacked these words and twisted them for their own gain. This is to say that the left often turns liberal, an ideology that in reality seeks to change or "improve" the US Constitution, into a word that means protecting America's Constitution, well, the parts they like, and the freedoms that come with it, at all costs, with special attention placed on those who have been historically marginalized; and as this pseudo-patriotism is occurring, on the other side of the aisle the right turns conservative, an ideology that in reality seeks to support the Constitution and all of the individual liberty that comes with it, into a word that means being in support of, essentially, a "religious theocracy" wherein America is run according to the Christian Bible. In other words, both parties have bastardized the meaning of these two words in order to appeal to their base and gain voters. So, shake off the definitions of liberal and conservative that you have been taught, and just remember that they really refer to change and no change with the US Constitution being the item at the center of this debate.

Ok, we have almost made it to the end of this chapter, but before we get to our sane position on partisanship, I just have a couple of final things to discuss. If you remember, earlier in this chapter I used the phrase "in theory" while discussing which side of the aisle each major US political party is on, and I also said that the reason I did this is because, according to my analyses, neither party, in their current forms, actually represents the conservative (right/no change) side of the left/right spectrum. Now I know this may seem like an outrageous statement to a lot of you out there but before you get too angry, stop and ask yourself what "conservative" actually means in relation to America's left/right divide, because in my summation it would mean maintaining the status quo, which as I have previously discussed is the US Constitution, a document centered around individual liberty and We the Peoples inherent power over the state. Well, aside from their carefully crafted speeches, which make them seem like they support right-wing values, can you truly say with confidence that *that* definition of maintaining the constitutional status quo looks like the Republican party today? Yeah, I didn't think so. I mean, maybe this is just some of my personal disdain for each of the parties bleeding through, but it is the case that the Republicans, who should be in favor of less government, have actually outspent the Democrats in recent years. Furthermore, the modern Republicans are responsible for the Patriot Act, which basically gives the government free reign to track our behavior, spy on us in our homes, and listen to everything we say. And, in addition to that, they recently were in support of the bipartisan Restrict Act, which, had it passed, would have essentially been like the Patriot Act on steroids. Oh yeah, and then there is also their nearly unanimous support for a new centralized US digital bank that issues government-controlled cryptocurrency. Are you starting to get the picture? I hope you are, but at any rate, I think that it is quite sane to say, at the very least, that the Republicans may not be Democrats, but according to a thorough study of the left/right continuum, as well as our founding documents, well, they sure as hell aren't right-wing conservatives either.

Now if you are like me, this revelation about both of our major parties technically being on the left side of the aisle makes you wonder if the system is still working. This is to say that given what we know about Duverger's law, won't the system be thrown out of balance if either side assumes too much power? Well, the answer to this question is yes, but there is a silver lining. You see, at this point in time it is my belief that the Republicans and Democrats, despite maintaining major differences in terms of specific policy preferences, have merged on the thesis, or left, side of the US political Hegelian Dialectic, which is a side that favors a large government, authoritarian-style political action, and religiously committed and sometimes radical followers. However, the right side has not been left vacant. Rather, on the right, or anti-thesis side of the US political Hegelian Dialectic, there now resides a growing subset of the population that opposes these leftist aspects of the two major parties and instead favors individual liberty. Of course, this faction does not currently have a party of its own but it does contain the politically homeless former moderates, the anarchists, the libertarians, and the citizens who are casually aware of what's going on and angry about it, but not explicitly political, all of whom could be a very powerful force if they were to unite. So, yes, right now the system is a bit out of whack, but with that said, we do appear to be in the midst of a pretty fundamental change, which, in my belief, will lead to the birth of an altogether new faction.

SIDENOTE

If this analysis of where we currently are is correct, and I think that the recent surge in the popularity of many anti-authority political action groups (Antifa, Mises Caucus, etc.), as well as the emergence and popularity of many liberty-focused media entities who were formerly left-wing (Tim Pool, Dave Reubin, etc.) suggest that it is, well, then this would mean that we could be on the verge of a new synthesis that is, hopefully, closer to the middle of the left/right continuum. Of course, we still have to see how all of this plays out over the next couple of decades, but nonetheless, I think it is clear that our political landscape is changing drastically, and with this change, we will see a true challenge to the two major parties. Or, at the very least, an increase in cultural pressures that forces both of them to move closer to the right, thus restoring balance to the entire winner take all system. Now maybe you still think that this view of where we are is crazy, but doesn't it make sense given how many people are now openly "fed up" with the two major parties? I'll leave you to ponder that during your own time because right now I need to wrap this thing up.

Alright, so the reason I bring all of this up is because, as I was writing this chapter I began to wonder if there is even a point in being sane about partisanship. This is to say that in my mind, I began to ask myself, "What's the point?" I mean, if my ballot is and always will be a vote cast for what I deem to be the lesser of two evils, and both of those are on the left anyway, then why waste time coming up with a nuanced position on this issue at all? Instead, why wouldn't I just pick the side that is closest to what I believe and then leave it at that? Well, I won't lie to you. Wielding our political power as citizens is not always an immediate and/or satisfying slam dunk because each vote by itself matters very little, and even then, there are only two choices, at least for now; but despite this fact you shouldn't lose hope. I say this because We the People still have many ways that we can, if we unite, influence the two major parties and have our voices heard. In other words, in lieu of resorting ourselves to this status quo of having a country run by two parties on the left, let us instead focus on what we can do to restore order to this system. Especially because, as I have shown, regardless of what side of the aisle you are on, maintaining balance is good for all of us. Anyway, let's close out this chapter by briefly discussing three ways that We the People can help return our parties to healthy positions on the left/right continuum, thus restoring balance to the system, and then by establishing a sane position on partisanship as a whole.

To begin, the first thing we can do as citizens, as trivial as it may seem, is to write to our elected leaders, or the candidates trying to unseat them. Now I know this sounds silly, but as someone with a Graduate degree in the field of Political Psychology, I can tell you that, as far-fetched as it may seem, political candidates and their administrations are desperate to hear from you. I mean, in 2020 alone the total cost of campaigns in the US was well over 10 billion US dollars, and a good bit of that was spent just trying to get a finger on the pulse of the electorate. So, in other words, right now your elected leaders, and their opposition, are both spending boatloads of cash trying to get your opinion so that they can learn how to court your vote. Ergo, it may not seem like much, but if enough of us let a candidate know that they are on thin ice and should pay more attention to (insert policy and/or issue), then we can influence their decision-making, just like the citizens did in regard to social justice in between 1860 and 1936.

Moving on, the second thing that we can do to have our sane voices heard is to organize community events. I know, I know, we all hate the endless stream of lunatics, on both sides mind you, walking down the street and chanting phrases that make no sense. But with that said, local movements do actually tend to get a lot of attention from the media since Americans, after all, have become obsessed with political drama. So, yes, as annoying as most of them are to watch, mainly because they generally attract the "crazies," local political events are still excellent avenues for drawing attention and/or influencing candidates.

Now the third and final way to influence change that I want to talk about is voting for a third party. In other words, instead of voting for a Republican or Democrat, even though one of those will almost certainly win, cast your vote for the third most likely option, or even just write in the option you feel best reflects your positions. Yeah, I know, it feels like you are throwing away your vote just thinking about doing this, but here is the thing. As I previously stated, billions of dollars are going into figuring out how you feel. Well, this level of analysis doesn't just stop after the election is over. Instead, after each cycle people who work in my field make tons of money conducting independent studies for candidates that aim to figure out what worked, and what didn't. So, if both party's candidates see that they had a record low turnout for their party because a third-party candidate won 10-20% of the vote, well, even though that third-party candidate didn't win, their success would certainly send a message that the people are not happy with the status quo. Make sense?

Alright everyone, this is the end of the chapter and since you know what the left/right continuum actually is, as well as how our two main political parties' factor into that continuum, and why, it is finally time to tell you what the sane position on partisanship is. Now this issue is a bit different from the other issues in this book in the sense that, technically it isn't an issue at all because I can't really tell you who the sane party is to vote for because the parties are always changing their positions. That, and neither party is actually all that sane to begin with. But regardless, in essence, the voters on the other side of you are not inherently evil, and if our winner take all system is functioning properly, you actually need them in order to maintain systemic balance and stability, which, in turn maintains your liberty. So, the "sane" position in regard to partisanship is to be an educated, sophisticated voter, not a tribalist, and to be civil with the other side, because, well, even though it is healthy to disagree with one another, on a structural level we are all still on the American side, even if it doesn't seem like it right now.

SIDENOTE

I know this answer may seem a bit obscure, but I felt that this chapter still needed to be included, and more specifically included at the beginning because if you are going through this book simply viewing politics in terms of a Republican/ Democrat binary, well, you probably won't get very much out of it. Of course, with that said, don't worry, from here on out the sane positions will be explicit and easy to understand. Anyway, I'll see you in the next chapter folks.

CHAPTER 3

Abortion

Abortion. What a strange word. I mean, technically this word should be just like any other three-syllable combination of four vowels and four consonants, but in modern-day America the word abortion is far from menial and instead is a word that inspires heated debates from both sides of the political aisle. If you don't believe me, just go to the next pro-choice or pro-life rally in your local area and you will be able to see with your own eyes the passion each side feels in regard to this issue. More than likely, if the event you go to is like its predecessors, you will immediately see two immense and diverse groups of angry people holding homemade signs and yelling at one another. One of these sides will be the left and they will be adamantly speaking against the other side and claiming that they want to oppress women and control their bodies. Across from them, with an equal amount of fervor in their tone, will be a group of right-leaning people declaring that all of those on the opposing side of the rally want to murder babies.

SIDENOTE

In the last chapter I discussed how the modern Republican Party is technically close to or even on the left side of America's political aisle. With this said, to keep things simple from here on out I will use the term *right* to distinguish people who align with the Republican Party and the term *left* to refer to people who align with the Democrat party. Yes, this is, at least in my summation, inaccurate, but since it has become normal within our cultural zeitgeist to call the Republicans right-wing and the Democrats left-wing, in order to keep you from getting confused I will do the same.

Let me ask you a question. If you were to go to one of these events, do you know which of the two sides you would be on? If you do, let me ask you why you chose that side. Was it because of your religion? Your personal experience with having children? Your personal experience with having abortions? Your personal experience with having both? Or is it because of your partisan alignment? Unfortunately, for a significant number of us I imagine this final option will end up being the answer. If I am right about this, and I hope I'm not, well, that is truly a shame. I say this because abortion, in all reality, shouldn't be a partisan issue at all. In fact, the issue really shouldn't even be all that political. This is because abortion, in essence, is a moral issue, not a policy one. Of course, with that said, policies, which then become laws, are technically how we enforce our societal standards of morality. So, I guess in that sense it is a policy debate. Anyway, regardless of what the abortion debate should be, this moral issue has been hijacked, much like some of the other issues in this book, by the two major parties and is instead now being wielded as a partisan weapon. Therefore, because of this unfortunate reality, we, the sane citizens, must be the ones to look at abortion objectively while putting our own personal party alliances aside in order to figure out what a reasonable position is on this issue that the US Constitution would approve of. Essentially, that is what this chapter aims to do. To begin, let's look at what abortion actually is, what the reasons for getting an abortion are, and some of its historical high notes, not only in the US but also in regard to human history as a whole. Then, after that, we will move on and talk about both sides of the current abortion debate, where the main friction point is in regard to these two positions, and last but not least what science has to say about this issue. All of which will lead to us finding a sane position on abortion. Good to go? Great.

According to Webster's dictionary abortion is "The termination of a pregnancy after, accompanied by, resulting in, or closely followed by the death of the embryo or fetus." Now right off the bat, it is important to note that the use of the word "termination" in this definition indicates that abortion is not a naturally occurring event like a miscarriage or stillbirth. Rather, termination means that someone is intentionally inducing the end of the pregnancy. This is to say that in no circumstance is an abortion natural.

Now why, you ask, would someone want to intentionally end a pregnancy? After all, having children is, evolutionarily speaking, our main reason for existence. Furthermore, having children seems like it has been a staple of a fulfilled life since, quite literally, the beginning of our species, and this has applied to every culture, not just the West mind you. Well, to help explain why this biologically counterintuitive practice exists let's start by talking about the four most prevalent rationales that pro-choice advocates use to explain why individuals choose to intentionally end their pregnancies because, despite our biological imperative to conceive, carry, bear, and foster children, abortions still happen, and a lot of them (nearly 700,000 in 2019 and 2020 according to the CDC and Guttmacher Institute).

Put plainly, abortions are induced in order to **1)** terminate a pregnancy that is the result of rape or incest, **2)** preserve the life or physical/mental well-being of the mother, **3)** to avoid a child being birthed that has either a genetic abnormality, serious deformity, or mental deficiency, and **4)** to keep a person who feels they cannot support a child, due to social or economic reasons such as extreme youth or a lack of resources, from having to carry the child to term. Pretty straightforward, right? Well, even though this is the case, if you are like me, you noticed that there is quite a bit of range when it comes to these rationales and though they are all easy to understand, not all of them, at face value, are created equal. Because of this let's go a little deeper and break them down separately so that we can more accurately discuss each one's validity when it comes to using them as a rationale for legalizing abortions nationwide.

Typically, at least in terms of US politics, the rationale of ending a pregnancy because of rape or incest is more or less unanimously agreed upon by both parties and is seen, even by the right side of the aisle, as justifiable. This also happens to be the one that the political left points to most often when making their pro-choice cases. Using this rationale as a justification to broadly accept abortion is somewhat of a strawman, however, because, statistically, this rationale for inducing an abortion is quite rare. In fact, most studies suggest that fewer than 1% of abortions are initiated for this reason. In other words, it really isn't a major factor in the overall abortion debate so using it to justify widespread legalization of abortion is the same as me driving a friend to the emergency room while intoxicated and then using that action, which everyone would agree needed to be done given the dire circumstances, as a rationale for broadly legalizing driving under the influence. Make sense?

The second rationale, which is also fairly commonly agreed upon by both sides of the aisle, is the one that has to do with the health of the mother, and like rape and incest, this too is also generally one of the top rationales that pro-choice advocates point to when fighting for their side. With that said, though, like the previously mentioned rationale this is also a bit of a strawman because the mental health of the mother is such an ambiguous standard. I mean, if a person says they will have a heightened level of anxiety if they go through with a pregnancy, technically speaking having an abortion could be medically justified as a form of preventative care that helps stabilize that person's mental health. Of course, even with this caveat, just so that we are being fair to the pro-choice side of the debate we are still going to keep the physical and mental health of the mother together as we discuss this second rationale.

Ok, so abortions that protect the physical health of the mother. Now, I do have to say that it is somewhat difficult to find sturdy statistics on this rationale, but the overwhelming consensus is that the number of abortions that are done to protect the life of the mother is still somewhere between 0% and 1%, and this is agreed upon by doctors on both sides of the debate. Here are two quotes that serve as evidence of this consensus.

"Today it is possible for almost any patient to be brought through pregnancy alive, unless she suffers from a fatal illness such as cancer or leukemia, and, if so, abortion would be unlikely to prolong, much less save, life."—Dr. Alan Guttmacher of Planned Parenthood

"Less than 1 percent of all abortions are performed to save the mother's life." —Dr. Landrum Shettles co-author of "From Conception to Birth: The Drama of Life's Beginnings."

Alright, if you need more than these two quotes feel free to look through the references, but for now, suffice it to say that, like the rape and incest rationale, saving the mother's life is also somewhat statistically irrelevant, thus making it a straw man if used to justify the legalization of abortion nationwide. In other words, due to its statistical insignificance, using this rationale to justify abortion nationwide would be like, to use the DUI example again, fighting to end all DUI laws across the country simply because of a few anecdotal instances wherein driving while intoxicated actually turned out to be the right course of action, which, we can all agree, is not only illogical, but also insane!

Of course, that is only half of this second rationale, isn't it? I mean, what about the mother's mental health? After all, we did say that in the spirit of fairness we would keep the two together, didn't we? Well, unfortunately, for pro-choice advocates at least, the mental health of the mother also appears to be a largely irrelevant rationale when it comes to the widespread legalization of abortion. Let me explain.

According to an analysis of official reports by liveaction.org, an analysis I carefully reviewed because, well, with a name like that you know they are biased, at most only about 1.3% of abortions are induced to preserve the mental health of the mother. Furthermore, according to research published in the Journal of Child Psychology and Psychiatry and BMC Medicine abortions do not even solve mental issues, and "in fact, often aggravate them." And in addition to this, research presented by the British Journal of Psychiatry concluded that "long-term mental health problems in the wake of induced abortions increase, and the probability of depression, anxiety, guilt, etc. goes up by 81% compared to mothers who carried their baby until birth. It is clear that mental health reasons worsen with abortion and compound the problem, rather than relieving such symptoms." Ergo, like rape and incest, as well as the physical health of the mother, abortion to preserve the mental health of a pregnant woman is not a valid rationale when it comes to explaining why the practice should be widely accepted.

Ok, so far we have established that two of these four rationales are already widely accepted by the right and also statistically irrelevant to the abortion debate at large. This indicates that even though they are typically the "go-to" of the pro-choice advocates, the main area of disagreement in regard to the abortion debate actually surrounds the other two rationales, which as I stated earlier are to avoid a child being birthed that possesses a genetic abnormality, serious deformity, or mental deficiency, and to keep a person who feels they cannot support a child, due to social or economic reasons such as extreme youth or a lack of resources, from having to carry the child to term. Furthermore, given the statistical irrelevance of these first two rationales, we can also conclude that the majority of modern abortions are performed for one of these latter two rationales. Now I am not going to entirely forget the first two rationales we covered, even if they are somewhat innocuous, but moving forward these latter two are going to be our *main* focus when it comes to finding a sane position on abortion because these latter two are the most prevalent.

So, on to the second two rationales. Now because we know that these two types of abortions make up the vast majority of abortions, instead of going into the specific statistics for these two rationales, I would rather spend our time discussing what makes them different from the former two. Sound like a plan?

SIDENOTE

Just so we are on the same page, the second two rationales are **3)** to avoid a child being birthed that has either a genetic abnormality, serious deformity, or mental deficiency, and **4)** to keep a person who feels they cannot support a child, due to social or economic reasons such as extreme youth or a lack of resources, from having to carry the child to term. I feel like these are pretty self-explanatory, but in case they aren't, the first is, essentially, when a doctor induces an abortion because the child is going to be disabled, and the second is, essentially, when a doctor induces an abortion because the mother can't afford to raise the child, and/or doesn't feel able to.

In essence, what makes these latter two rationales different is that these two rationales (**3,4**) are what I would describe as elective abortions. Yes, I know, I literally just said that abortion is not natural in any circumstance and "termination" is an active step that applies to all abortions, but given the extreme nature of situations that involve rape, incest, and/or the mother's health, I do not view those rationales the same as, say, a person choosing to terminate a healthy pregnancy simply because they do not feel like having a child. Therefore, much like how a quadruple bypass and a boob job do not possess the same level of gravitas, despite both being surgeries, these latter two rationales for inducing an abortion can be looked at more like cosmetic procedures rather than life-saving ones. Alright, with that said, before actually getting into these latter two rationales, which as I said before are the main points of disagreement surrounding the abortion debate, and also our main focus when it comes to finding a sane position on this issue, let's first take a step back and briefly look at the history of abortion so that we can better understand the practice as a whole and establish if this debate is relatively new, or if it has been around a while. Capeesh?

So when it comes to the history of abortion, I suppose that, theoretically, the best place to start would be at the very beginning. Unfortunately, though, despite only being a fragment of the overall history of the universe, humanity's history is much too long and much too dense to be adequately covered in this chapter, even if we are just talking about the parts of it that relate specifically to abortion. Ergo, despite the practice's long and thorough history, instead of doing a true blue deep dive on abortion we are instead just going to hit a few of the notable wavetops.

To begin, two paragraphs ago I said that we would find out if abortion is a relatively new practice. Put plainly, it isn't. In fact, as it turns out as early as 1550 BC the Egyptians were inducing abortions and the practice was so common in their culture that they even went so far as to put instructions about how to perform one in their medical texts. One example of this is the *Ebers Papyrus*, which is an ancient Egyptian medical text that actually told ancient Egyptian readers, in more detail than I care to share here, how to use plant fiber, honey, and even dates to terminate unwanted pregnancies. So yeah, people were having abortions even as far back as thirty-five hundred years ago. Ancient abortions didn't stop there though. This is to say that flash forward a few hundred years from the Egyptians and you find the Greeks and Romans, who were highly advanced civilizations for their time, also engaging in the practice of abortion. Evidence of this in Greece includes a quote by the famous Greek philosopher

Aristotle himself who said, on the topic of abortion, "When couples have children in excess, let abortion be procured before sense and life have begun." In other words, Aristotle, who was in no way alone in this belief (look through the references if you don't believe me), thought that the practice of abortion served as a great way to control the population…. pretty eerie stuff, right? Anyway, the Greeks were not alone in their views on abortion. This is to say that the mighty Romans were also similarly lax on the issue and only viewed abortion as an issue if the father felt he had been deprived of a child. In other words, abortions in ancient Rome were not necessarily seen as a homicide, but rather as a domestic crime that challenged a father's right to carry on his lineage.

SIDENOTE

Even though we have not established that every single ancient society freely performed abortions, we can pretty confidently deduce that their prevalence within these advanced ancient societies probably meant they were also being performed in the more primitive societies. Ergo, abortion was likely rather common, even as far back as a few thousand years ago.

There are other examples of ancient societies performing abortions, some of which are even found in the Bible of all places (Numbers 5: 11-31), but for parsimony let's move on to the AD side of human history, shall we? On this more modern side of history, many cultures have used abortions as well. Two major examples of this that my research led me to were the Japanese and the Chinese, and records show that these two nations started normalizing the practice sometime around the 12 century for Japan, and the 16th century for China. Now by this time ancient practices like squatting over a boiling pot of onions, which is a thing that ancient people really did and not a joke, became a thing of the past, and instead, modern abortions typically involved the use of potent and easy-to-make medicinal compounds that would remove "menstrual blockages." Of course, how common and/or taboo getting one of these chemical abortions was in these societies is difficult to tell from the historical record alone, but nonetheless, their existence at all does show that the practice didn't die in ancient times as one may have assumed but rather continued to be a studied practice among civilized societies at least until after humanity moved into the modern era (post-1500 AD).

SIDENOTE

An interesting side note about Japan and China during this timeframe is that even though both of these societies accepted abortion, in Japan the majority of these procedures were performed on the peasant class, a class that had trouble supporting themselves during this period due to famines and very high taxes from the emperor, while over in China abortion was instead one of the benefits of being wealthy. This is to say that, sure, Chinese peasants, such as prostitutes, for instance, still commonly performed chemical abortions on themselves, which is something that we can assume has been a norm for women in that line of work throughout all of human history, but what is unique about 16th-century China is that the royal women were actually the ones regularly getting abortions, not the peasant class. Now as to why they were the ones choosing to get abortions over the peasant class is up for debate, perhaps it was to protect bloodlines, hide relations that occurred out of wedlock, or just simple family planning, but nonetheless, I just thought this was an interesting factoid that demonstrates how two societies who were okay with abortion viewed it in two totally different ways; thus showing the complexity of applying uniform abortion laws to a gigantic and very ideologically diverse population like that of the United States. Anyway, let's move on.

Ok, so that wasn't the whole history of abortion, but hopefully it was enough to convey to you the point that abortion is not at all new. In fact, during my research for this chapter, I was a little surprised to find out just how cheap all human life has been for the majority of our history, not just infant life. I mean, even beyond abortion, suffice it to say that if you were a bastard prior to the post-modern era, well, you better damn well have watched your back because you were not looked kindly upon by society and very likely would have been killed. I digress though. Now that you have a rough idea of the history of abortion, in the context of the human species as a whole, that is, it is now time to talk specifically about the history of abortion in America. Now, again, because of space constraints, I just want to hit the wavetops, but for all the nerds out there, don't worry, the references section is still there for you if you want to know more.

All right, time to talk about abortion in America. Now this may be surprising to some of you out there given that the United States is seen as a predominantly Christian nation, a group that has pretty much been against all abortion since 313 AD when the Catholic church proclaimed that any woman who intentionally ends a pregnancy is guilty of murder, but until the early 17th-century abortion was actually largely unregulated in our country. I say largely because the cultural norm at the time was that abortion was ok up until "quickening" had occurred, a term that refers to when the child can be felt moving within the womb, which typically happens around the second trimester, and therefore was not totally accepted. At any rate, though, despite the lack of abortion legislation present in our early days, things began to change somewhat quickly after Connecticut became the first state to officially make performing an abortion a criminal offense in 1821.

Now, in a way this Connecticut legislation got the ball rolling in terms of the pro-life movement back in the day, but that movement didn't truly pick up a significant amount of national steam until Dr. Horatio Storer, a gynecologist and staunch anti-abortion activist, published his book entitled *The Hand-Book of Domestic Medicine* in 1855; a book that, among other things, used previously unheard-of terms like "emmenagogues," which are substances that provoke uterine bleeding for the purpose of terminating a pregnancy, and many more pro-life terms that were new for the time, many of which somewhat shocked the populace. In other words, this written work, as well as Storers' activism, resonated deeply with a population that, if you remember the last chapter, was growing ever more concerned with human rights at the time, and this cultural concern combined with his political efforts ended up kicking the abortion debate into high gear for the first time in the US.

Moving on, recognizing the need to take full advantage of this cultural momentum, just two years later in 1857 Storer started a nationwide pro-life movement that would come to be known as the Physicians' Crusade Against Abortion; and to put it lightly, this organization, which was made up of a coalition of doctors and subject matter experts who sought to ban abortion in the US is still heralded by many pro-life activists as the main reason we have a pro-life movement today. Let me explain.

You see, the reason many modern pro-life advocates see the Physicians' Crusade Against Abortion as such an important linchpin in the pro-life movement is because this entity became so powerful at the time that they actually drove the federal government to do things like pass the 1873 Comstock Act. Now by getting this act passed, the stated objective of which was to ban the mailing of obscene and immoral material, to include information on abortion-causing substances and "how-to" material, the Physicians' Crusade Against Abortion had also laid the groundwork for, very shortly thereafter, all of the states in America to actually outlaw abortion outright. So, essentially, thanks to the efforts of this organization, within 50 years America had gone from not discussing abortion at all on the national stage to banning it outright. Thus making them, to this day, heroes within the pro-life movement.

SIDENOTE

Not saying that I agree with an outright ban on abortion, but it is pretty wild the power one group of people can have when they have the culture on their side, isn't it? Just food for thought for those of you who feel that We the People are incapable of instigating change. Anyway….

Skipping ahead a bit, this status quo of abortions being federally illegal remained the case for nearly a hundred years, although with that said there is credible speculation that given the levels of poverty within the country during the great depression, abortion laws were not always strictly enforced. At any rate, though, in the mid-late 18th century Planned Parenthood, an organization started by Margaret Sanger in 1921 (originally called the American Birth Control League), started to revive the abortion debate within the country, and in 1955 they held a conference in New York entitled "Abortion in the United States." Now this small conference, despite how little press it got at first, was actually a significant step in the birth of the modern pro-choice movement because this particular conference was the first-ever national conference focused on abortion in the history of the US, and it was effective. This is to say that by the time the record of this conference was published and widely distributed, roughly three years later, the record, which contained testimony from pro-choice sex researchers and pro-choice doctors, to put it frankly, made a massive cultural splash. Ergo, much like Dr. Storer's work in the mid-19th century had quickly gained national prominence, this pro-choice ideological splash infected the entire country and wasted no time in moving the needle forward for the pro-abortion side of the debate; and as a result of this new cultural pressure, soon thereafter some states, such as California (1963), Colorado (1963), Hawaii (1970), and New York (1970) began to reject the longstanding federal bans on abortion and instead decided to make their own decisions about the issue.

Now even though this 1960s period saw many states working to reject the federal abortion bans and instead make abortions safe and easily accessible, things really began to heat up around the abortion debate in 1971 when the case we by now have probably all heard about, Roe V Wade, went before the Supreme Court. To summarize, in this case, Jane Roe, whose real name was Norma McCorvey, was an unmarried pregnant woman from Texas who challenged the Texas state law preventing abortions except in cases where they were medically necessary to save the mother. Well, as I said before, this battle made it all the way to the supreme court and was waged for three years. Now we don't have time to get into all of the intricacies of that case, but it is sufficient to say that, eventually, the Roe side won and abortion was legalized federally across all fifty states, thus making it the greatest pro-choice victory to date, and, up until very recently, the status quo. In other words, there have been a few major battles between the pro-choice side and pro-life side post-Roe V Wade, a notable of which is the battle over the legality of partial-birth abortions, but all in all, since that 1973 decision abortions have been, at least until recently, legal, and accessible no matter where you are in the continental United States.

Ok, so that is a brief rundown of the history of abortion, and specifically its history in the US. Well, now it is finally time to move to the fun part, at least for me. This is to say that we are finally up to our current day and age and can now begin to discuss how the abortion debate currently looks on the political landscape, as well as what a sane position is in regard to this issue, which, as a political analyst I find very interesting. So, without further to do, let's get into it.

In June 2022 the Supreme Court, after nearly fifty years of upholding Roe V Wade voted to overturn the longstanding ruling. Of course, this decision, though a big win for the pro-lifers, did not make abortion federally illegal again, but it did however give the power to make abortion legislation back to the states. Well, because this is the case and the federal government has removed itself from the abortion debate, we cannot now, in our modern day and age, simply look at the abortion debate as one singular debate, as we would have back in the day; rather, it is now 50 individual debates that occur on a state-by-state basis. With this said, though, since we know that the government is not opposed to making federal-level laws in regard to the practice, and also that We the People bear a responsibility to wield our political power on the state level just as much as we have a responsibility to do so on the federal level, we here in this book will continue to talk about the abortion debate in a broad, national context, not a state-by-state one. The reason for this is that I want you, a member of that aforementioned active citizenry, to have a sane position on abortion regardless of *where* you physically reside within the United States. Plus, just as a bonus, should the federal government ever change its mind and decide to get involved again, which it likely will, I want you to be prepared for that political landscape as well.

Ok, moving on, even though each state has its own unique laws and policies regarding abortion, the two major parties that run this country have been pretty open about their overarching national agendas when it comes to the practice. This is to say that the Democrat faction, it would seem, has reached the conclusion that abortions, including elective abortions, should be legal up until the point of birth, and some of them, such as Virginia's former governor Ralph Northam even believe that there should be provisions for "after-birth" abortions. Of course, this last position, though growing in popularity among the Democrats, for right now is still on the fringes of the left. Therefore, we will simply say that elective abortions up until the point of birth is the general consensus among the majority of the party.

Now the Republican faction, on the other hand, seems to have the complete opposite stance on abortion. This is to say that even though most of them have only pushed for heartbeat bills so far, which make abortions illegal after a heartbeat has been detected, the overall goal of the party appears to be outlawing all abortions from the point of conception. Of course, this stance is obviously a difficult one to argue without using religion, something the government is not

Constitutionally permitted to do, so that is likely why, as of right now, they are currently stuck using a heartbeat as their standard. Ergo, we will simply say that the overarching Republican position on abortion is to ban them after a heartbeat has been detected.

SIDENOTE

In this book, I do not want to appear too militant towards those who are religious, in particular the Christians, but I do want to be very clear about why we cannot use religion to make laws. Now I recognize that this will likely not be something some of you want to hear because you have been conditioned by phrases like, "This is a Christian nation," or "The founders were influenced by Judeo-Christian values," but to be blunt, these phrases are mostly just non-starters and/or substance less catchphrases that have been used by politicians and pundits alike to get your support by playing on your faith. In other words, we are not a Christian nation, and the idea that our country should be governed by Christian doctrines is false. Let me explain.

First off, Britain was a Christian country, so the idea that Christianity is what makes our country unique is false. Furthermore, the individuals who fled Britain to come to this country did so a full 150 years before the Declaration of Independence was authored. Ergo, regardless of why those first settlers came here, presumably for religious reasons, that action actually had very little if anything to do with the founders and/or our Constitution.

Second off, many of the founders were either not Christians at all or not the type of Christians that the modern religious right likes to pretend they were. This is to say that some were atheists, such as Benjamin Franklin, some were deists, like Thomas Payne who openly stated that he believed the Christian Bible was a barbaric and cruel document more likely written by a demon than by God, and some were Christians, but again, not by the religious rights standards of Christianity. I.e., Thomas Jefferson, for instance, wrote an entire Bible that excluded anything supernatural because he thought all of that was nonsense and folly, and he did this as a "Christian."

The third, and arguably the most important of the reasons why we are not a Christian nation, is that the First Amendment (keep in mind amendments are additions to the Constitution, not corrections) is very clear about how much religion should influence legislation. "**Congress shall make no law respecting an establishment of religion**, *or prohibiting the free exercise thereof; or abridging the freedom of speech, or of the press; or the right of the people peaceably to assemble, and to petition the Government for a redress of grievances.*" In lay terms, none.

Ok, so now that we know the overarching positions of the two parties when it comes to abortion, it is safe to say that, considering that these two positions are rather far removed from one another, we, the sane citizens, are left with quite a large ideological area to search if we are to find where the main disagreement is. Well, fret not because, luckily for you, I have already searched this wasteland of possible positions and found an answer. This is to say that after studying the written arguments by scholars on both sides of the divide I have concluded that the main disagreement, AKA the main source of friction when it comes to the abortion debate is simple. Where does life begin?

Now if one is not careful the search for an answer to this seemingly simple question can send that person, as it did me, down an endless rabbit hole of moral philosophy. Well, unfortunately, though that road is interesting, it is also a road that doesn't really lead anywhere tangible. Therefore, after realizing how abstract those arguments were, as well as how little empirical evidence they provide (As a man of science I do not find arguments about the soul compelling.), I actually decided that a better way to determine what constitutes a life, and subsequently what a sane stance on abortion is, was to change directions away from moral philosophy and instead figure out what constitutes a legal death. You see, in my mind, working backward from this point, a point founded in medicine, would not only help me find out how the law views life, but also what a constitutionally sound position on abortion legislation is because even though the Constitution does not specifically mention the procedure, it is pretty clear about *people* having an inherent right to engage in life, liberty, and the pursuit of happiness. In other words, if a citizen can be legally killed, then they are alive. Furthermore, if a citizen is alive, then they also have Constitutional rights, one of which is a right to life, and these Constitutional rights apply to anyone here who is legally alive, *even* if they are yet to be born. So, with that said, when is someone dead, and what does this tell us about where life begins?

To begin, I can't speak for other countries, but here in the United States we have something called the Uniform Determination of Death Act (UDDA), and according to this act, there are officially two types of legal death. Now the first, which is known as cardiopulmonary death, is, essentially, when a doctor determines that a patient is experiencing irreversible cessation of circulatory and respiratory functions, which means that the heart has stopped and the patient is not breathing on their own, and subsequently declares that patient legally dead. In other words, a person can be declared legally dead after their heart has stopped, and/or their breathing has stopped, and there is no chance they will return. Pretty simple, right?

The second type of legal death, however, is referred to as brain death, and in these instances, a doctor can pronounce a patient dead if they have determined that the patient is experiencing irreversible cessation of all functions of the entire brain, including the brain stem, regardless of whether or not the heart is still functioning. In other words, if the brain activity has reached a certain point of decline, then a doctor can pronounce that person dead, even though their body may actually be fine. Now, there is still some debate when it comes to the exact line for this second type of death, mainly because many people still argue that a person who is only partially brain-dead should be considered fully brain-dead, but I won't get into these debates because the US standard for declaring someone brain dead, as it stands now, is total brain death. Good to go?

Alright, so we know now what makes someone legally dead, and therefore what should make them legally alive. But when it comes to abortion which of these two types of death should we actually use to determine when someone is legally alive? Well, at this point in time, we know that the brain, including the brain stem, is pretty much fully developed around the end of the second trimester, which, for those who aren't familiar with pregnancy, is around the six-month mark. Ergo, because of this we can be fairly certain that an otherwise healthy child, regardless of whether they are still in the uterus or not, should be legally considered alive by the end of the second trimester. In other words, this means that any abortions performed after this stage of pregnancy are not sane because they would, essentially, be proactively initiating a brain death. But what about the other legal standard of life and death?

Well, when it comes to cardiopulmonary death, the common consensus within the medical community is that a fetal heartbeat can be picked up by an ultrasound machine at six weeks, though there is some debate about whether or not this truly constitutes a heartbeat. This is to say that some doctors believe that even though the cardiac tissue is technically beating at the six-week mark, the heart is technically not fully developed until around the ninth or tenth week of pregnancy, which leaves us, the rational citizens trying to form a sane position on abortion, in a bit of a pickle. Well, I don't know about you, but I feel that a good way to solve this pickle is to ask ourselves what we would do with an adult patient who has a defective heart and/or a birth defect. In other words, do we consider them to be alive, or if they are on the operating table do one of the attending physicians look around the room and go, "Time of death…. well they were already dead, sooooooo?" Of course not! Therefore, despite the fact that the heart is not fully matured at six weeks, it appears to me that the logical and sane solution to this ethical pickle is to consider the six-week heartbeat the official standard of legal cardiopulmonary life in infants. Sorry pro-choicers. If it helps, I was hoping you guys would be right. I digress though.

SIDENOTE

Notice that this conclusion renders the second type of death irrelevant to our abortion debate since the potential for brain death happens far later than when the potential for cardiopulmonary death exists. In other words, if a fetus/embryo makes it to the stage where brain death can be induced, the heartbeat has already given that fetus/embryo validity and made it, technically, a legal life.

Furthermore, to those who are going to say that this conclusion is incorrect because, technically, a fetus should be considered brain dead before the end of the second trimester, well, that is actually incorrect. You see, in order for brain death to be pronounced the fetus would have to experience irreversible cessation of all functions of the entire brain, including the brain stem. Put plainly, this is not the case when the brain is simply "not developed." I.e., yes, the fetus has not technically experienced brain life by the time the heartbeat has started, but in time it will. Ergo, the lack of brain activity at this stage does not constitute an irreversible cessation of all functions of the entire brain, including the brain stem, and therefore does not override the fact that, at this stage, the fetus *has* experienced cardiopulmonary life.

So, there it is everyone, the answer to where legal life begins. In other words, it would appear that a sane citizen, regardless of their political party and/or personal religious beliefs, should view ending a pregnancy after the heartbeat has been established (again, generally around six weeks) as unethical since this would technically be meeting the criteria of actively inducing a cardiopulmonary death. Of course, saying that this is a sane position still feels a little funny because I know that it is very likely that most of you out there will still disagree with it. But nonetheless, I am ok with that because regardless of whether you disagree because of your party allegiance or the religious doctrine you follow, this book is not being written to appease you. Rather, it is being written so that we can find out where both sides disagree on these particular issues, and then what the objectively sane position is on them, which I feel confident that I have done.

SIDENOTE

Now I don't want to beat a dead horse here, but to the people who still disagree with my sane position, I just want to explain why I cannot accept the conception argument and/or the point of birth argument. Put plainly, using the conception argument as the standard the government should follow for abortion laws, regardless of the existence of unique DNA and/or fetal potential, just isn't a logical enough standard since, as it stands now, this is not a standard we use to legally determine death. Furthermore, I also cannot accept the pro-choice arguments for elective abortions up until the point of birth because, put plainly, according to the legal standard of life and death elective abortions after the infant is legally alive are not abortions that are saving one life over the other, but are instead ending one life simply for the sake of the other's convenience. Now I know that is a bit blunt, but if having a nicer car would drastically improve my quality of life, as well as my subsequent mental health, I still cannot legally kill someone and take their vehicle; and this is true even if that person has a heart defect, terminal lung cancer, a learning disability, or any other ailment that makes them technically "less viable" than the average person. Make sense?

Ok folks, that is it, the end of the chapter. I know some will call my stance a far-right one and others will call it a markedly liberal one, but in closing let me just say this. If you can find a fault in my logic, so be it. However, if you disagree with me because of your own personal beliefs, ask yourself this. Do you want a country that is governed by the whims of whoever is in charge? Or, like me, would you rather have a country that forces its leaders to adhere to its founding documents and objective reality so that no one person can ever become a tyrant who forces us all to live by their arbitrary standards? In other words, would you rather have a sane position be the policy standard, even if it is a position neither side fully agrees with, or do you want to break down the barriers between personal belief and Constitutional law so that you can roll the dice and maybe get a dictator in power who thinks just like you? Just food for thought.

Anyway, I'll end my Libertarian-style rant there. In closing, for real this time, I hope you enjoyed the chapter and even learned a thing or two. Even if you did, though, still question everything I said and do your own analyses because you, like me, are also charged with helping direct the political power of the United States, and/or wielding We the People's power in a way that influences our leaders to implement policy positions that are not only sane but also ones that align with our beautiful Constitution. Got it? Alright, see you in the next chapter everyone wherein we will be discussing marriage.

Marriage

Initially, I entitled this chapter "Same-Sex Marriage." The reason for this is that this seemed to me, at the time, to make the most sense for a title because same-sex marriage is really the only type of marriage people in the US still disagree on. I mean, sure, in the past interracial marriage has been a point of contention on the national debate stage, and I would wager that in the future things like inter-species marriage will be on the docket, but for right now gay marriage is the hot topic when it comes to marriage laws. Of course, with this said, however, as you have no doubt noticed I have since changed the title simply to "Marriage" because after delving into the topic of same-sex marriage I realized that it is impossible to discuss this issue without also talking about the institution of marriage as a whole, which, as it turns out, is a topic that is much broader and more complex than I had anticipated. Anyway, when it was all said and done and my research was complete the new title worked much better because, despite this chapter being primarily focused on same-sex marriages, much of my research actually consisted of topics that were not explicitly related to that topic at all.

Now the reason I am telling you all of this here at the beginning is because, as we go through this chapter, I didn't want you to either lose sight of the purpose of said chapter, to find a sane position on same-sex marriage, or to get frustrated by the fact that it takes me a minute or two to get to that section. Make sense? Great.

Alright, now that I have addressed these concerns and you, for the most part, know what's what, if there are no objections let's look at what marriage actually is and where it comes from, a brief history of the practice in the US, how same-sex marriage ties into that history, and finally, what the US government's role in regulating it should be, if any. Then, we will finish up by determining what a sane position on this issue should be. Sound like a plan? Very well. To begin, let's start things out by first finding a tangible definition of what marriage means that you and I can use throughout the rest of the chapter, and then by establishing why people get married in the first place.

When it comes to what marriage actually is, my deep dive, as the previous paragraph suggests, started with the basics, which, if I am being honest consisted of me sitting at my dining room table typing "What is marriage" into Google. Well, shortly thereafter I was directed to the always reliable Webster's Dictionary, a source I have grown quite fond of during the course of writing this book, and according to this source marriage is **a)** the state of being united as spouses in a consensual and contractual relationship recognized by law **b)** the mutual relation of married persons—Wedlock **c)** the institution whereby individuals are joined in a marriage.

Now this three-part definition does technically work, and it certainly helped get the ball rolling, however, it truly is "the basics" as far as definitions for marriage go because, put frankly, these definitions, though seemingly obvious and self-evident, are really rather ambiguous.

In other words, they say it all without really saying anything. Ergo, after making this disappointing realization I decided to continue my search in hopes that I would find another, more useable definition, and this follow-on search eventually led me, as it very often does, to Britannica, whose alternate definition of marriage is as follows:

> *"Marriage—a legally and socially sanctioned union, usually between a man and a woman, that is regulated by laws, rules, customs, beliefs, and attitudes that prescribe the rights and duties of the partners and accords status to their offspring (if any). The universality of marriage within different societies and cultures is attributed to the many basic social and personal functions for which it provides structure, such as sexual gratification and regulation, division of labor between the sexes, economic production and consumption, and satisfaction of personal needs for affection, status, and companionship. Perhaps its strongest function concerns procreation, the care of children and their education and socialization, and the regulation of lines of descent. Through the ages, marriages have taken a great number of forms. (Exchange marriage; group marriage; polyandry; polygamy; tree marriage, and common-law marriage.)"*

Alright, now that is a definition we can chew on for a minute or two. Essentially, what it says is that the reason people marry one another is because there are actually quite a few personal benefits associated with the practice. But what are these benefits? Well, let's find out.

One of the personal benefits of marriage is an economic benefit and it can be manifested in several different ways. For instance, marriage, if used wisely, can be used to increase ones overall net worth and/or quality of life by fostering **A)** dual-income households wherein two working partners share one living space, **B)** single income households wherein one partner tends to the home (and/or children) while the other focuses on collecting wealth/resources, **C)** economically beneficial family alliances (i.e., two elites securing a strategic political alliance through the union of their children, a person of low economic status "marrying up" into a family with high economic status, etc.), and more recently, **D)** tax breaks/incentives passed down by the federal government.

The second and third personal benefits of participating in the practice of marriage are the psychological and physical benefits one gets whilst in Wedlock, and these types of benefits are the ones that most of us would say are self-evident, or even obvious, because they are inherently tied to several biological drives that all of us regularly experience. This is all to say that, put frankly, humans are social creatures, as well as horny creatures, and for many people marriage conveniently solves both of these needs at once. Now of course people do not necessarily have to be married to do these things, and I recognize that, but nonetheless, according to decades of research it is a fact that marriage does, from a technical perspective, fulfill and sustain these needs better than intimate relationships that have lower levels of commitment do. Ergo, marriage is not necessary to have sex/companionship, but generally speaking you will have higher quality sex and/or companionship if you have a spouse. Anyway, we will dig into that stuff a little more in a bit, but for now, let's get to the final and arguably most foundational benefit of marriage.

SIDENOTE

Technically speaking there are an unlimited number of reasons to get married because what people get out of the practice varies from person to person and from couple to couple. So, when I say that this next benefit is the final one, I simply mean that it is the final in *my* list of general personal benefits. In other words, don't get all up in arms just because I did not describe *your* specific scenario.

Alright, the final benefit of getting married is what I would describe as an evolutionary one, not a social one, and this benefit is important because at the end of the day it underlies and/or ties into all of the other benefits. In other words, it is quite literally, from a scientific perspective, the foundation for the other benefits. Let me explain what I mean by that. If you remember the beginning of the last chapter then you remember that I posed the question, "Why would someone want to intentionally end a pregnancy?" and this was followed by "After all, having children is, evolutionarily speaking, our main reason for existence. This is to say that propagating our genes and passing them on is, essentially, the main reason we are here, at least from a cold and scientific perspective." Sound familiar? Well, it should, but either way you can trust that I was not lying when I made these follow-on statements.

You see, having children is obviously a natural behavior. I mean, can you name one living organism that doesn't reproduce. I didn't think so. At any rate, though, my point is that the academic data overwhelmingly supports the idea that, from an evolutionary biology perspective, our primary reason for existing is to procreate because this allows our genes to continue on and evolve. Well, continuing along those same lines, given that this is our evolutionary purpose it would certainly make sense that human behavior would evolve to support this function, correct? Indeed, that is correct and from this realization it is very easy to see that, in a way, this is what marriage is. In other words, in essence marriage is an evolutionarily inspired behavior designed to aid in/support the creation and fostering of children, which, at the end of the day is us simply passing on our genetic code. At least from a technical perspective that is; but I digress, though, because I imagine right now some of you may be wondering how marriage specifically, as a behavior, actually does this in the first place. I.e., how can I say the practice of marriage is an evolutionarily developed behavior designed to aid in the propagation of our genes if humans can and do procreate without it, and isn't it just as likely that it is a learned behavior from our cultural environment and not a natural one stemming from our evolution? Good question.

SIDENOTE

The reason that the evolutionary benefit of marriage (it assists with passing on our genes) underlies all the rest is because, well, think about it. All of the other reasons for getting married (I.e., money, political reasons, etc.) all have to do with increasing your life's length/quality, which, presumably, you are driven to do because these increase your chances of successfully passing on your genes. Ergo, in some way or another, at the end of the day everything comes back to our biological design.

The answer to that good question you just asked is something called paternal certainty, and this term is exactly what it sounds like. I.e., if a man is certain that the children he is raising are biologically his, then he has paternal certainty, and this is, evolutionarily speaking, important because if he has this, he then knows that any investment he makes in those children is an investment that serves his own inherent biological drive to pass on his genes. Now as to how this all ties into marriage, well, in order to have paternal certainty the man must ensure that he is the only one his mate is sleeping with. Otherwise, any children she has could, potentially, be someone else's. But how does he do this? I mean, wouldn't a woman just move on to another, more qualified mate if she feels like it? After all, *she* knows which children are hers regardless of who she is with. So, what's her evolutionary incentive for being monogamous?

Well, the father is not the only one who benefits from having a monogamous relationship. This is to say that, in return for giving the man paternal certainty with monogamy, the female mate, historically, would receive his protection and resources. In other words, he would give her a paternal investment, which in the long run would increase her children's chances of reaching adulthood, especially in the past when supermarkets and modern medicine were not so readily available. Ergo, if two mates agree to commit to one another, in say a marriage, for instance, well, the male mate gets what he needs, paternal certainty, and the female mate gets what she needs, resources.

To summarize, as we can see, the quid pro quo of forming a monogamous single-mate pair bond (marriage) supports our most basic evolutionary purpose (having children) by motivating each of the mates in that equation to make an investment in the mental and physical well-being of the other. This then increases each of their abilities to pass on their genes by increasing their chances of successfully bearing and raising healthy offspring. Ergo, with all of that said, it is reasonable to conclude that marriage is, in the most primal and/or basic sense, an evolutionarily inspired behavior that we developed in order to increase our chances of having strong, healthy children that make it to adulthood, which benefits us by allowing us to fulfill our primary evolutionary purpose.

Now I know that this explanation of the final reason we get married may seem like it takes all of the magic out of the whole ordeal, but don't be so glum. You see, sure, when we get married, at the end of the day we are just animals following our biological imperatives (and this applies to literally everything we do mind you), but that doesn't mean we don't make it fun. This is to say that much like how we have given eating, a basic biological function, a great deal of flair (dinner parties, cheat meals, celebratory feasts, etc.), for thousands of years humans have been making this natural quid pro quo between the sexes something special. Thus, the behavior of getting married, regardless of its actual origin point, is not just a basic biological function for our species anymore. Rather, we have turned it into a time-honored celebration. Of course, this chapter is not about the societal evolution of marriage practices, so I won't be getting into how every individual culture has put its own tasteful spin on it, but I just felt I needed to add in that addendum to keep any of you from getting too nihilistic. Anyway, now that I have, hopefully, avoided letting this chapter black pill anyone, I suppose I had better get back on track. With that said, let's move on and narrow our focus in on figuring out what a Constitutionally sound and sane position is in regard to marriage, and specifically same-sex marriage. Sound like a plan? Sweet.

SIDENOTE

As you can probably already guess, same-sex marriage, unlike heterosexual marriage, does not fulfill our primary evolutionary purpose (passing on our genes). Yet, gay couples still exist. Well, if you are wondering if this seemingly dichotomous reality breaks apart the whole evolutionary explanation and instead supports the idea that marriage is primarily a socially inspired practice, it doesn't. This is to say that, put frankly, same-sex couples are an evolutionary anomaly in the same way asexual people and infertile people are an evolutionary anomaly. Now, I know how this sounds, basically that I believe all of these people are evolutionary mistakes, but this isn't what I mean and certainly not how I would frame it because I hold no negative feelings toward homosexual people. Instead, I am simply saying that, evolutionarily speaking, some wires got crossed in the sexual development of same-sex people, just like a person who, again, is born sterile or asexual. Ergo, because of this they are, technically speaking, a deviation from the evolutionarily inspired norm; and the fact that they have been excluded from being involved in marriage throughout history, in which marriage was primarily about having children, is evidence of this. Of course, with that said many societies have been very open toward, and even celebratory of same-sex relationships, however, even in these societies same-sex relationships were still seen as inherently different than marriages. So, despite how my evolutionary explanation of "Why people marry" looks at face value, it does still hold up, we just have to recognize that nature has some quirks (man, it is hard not to sound homophobic when talking about this topic). Anyway, this might seem like a pointless sidenote right now, but trust me, this information will be relevant when we start to get into subjects like how our reasons for getting married in the West have evolved and/or changed over the last 200 years. So, just keep it in the back of your mind if you develop doubts.

Ok, moving on. At this point we know what marriage is, how it is beneficial, and also how it is a natural part of our evolution as a species. So, what's next? Well, instead of going through every culture's unique history when it comes to marriage practices, I want to instead focus specifically on the modern-era West. The reason for this is that the modern West, around the late 20th century, decided to do marriage a little bit differently from its predecessors and this is the framework we are living under currently. This is to say that, even though the underlying reason for marriage's existence in the modern West still comes from the same origin point as other cultures (increasing a couple's chances of successfully raising biological children), how we actually choose our marriage companions here in the United States has, in fact, changed quite a bit over the last couple hundred years. And since you and I live in the modern West, this change is notable when it comes to finding a sane position on marriage-related issues. So, without further to do, let's discuss how we here in that modern West see marriage today, and how this is different from how we did in the past.

In essence, up until the late 20th century marriage was more often than not seen by societies (including Western ones) as more of a business partnership than a profession of two people's love. This is to say that in these societies' marriages were either arranged, typically by the parents, in-group elders, or the political elites, or they were formed by two independent people who believed that there was a political and/or economic advantage to getting hitched. In lay terms, in these marriages function came first and love came later. Well, during the late 20th century the West actually changed this cultural norm and subsequently started to view marriage as a thing people did only after they had fallen for one another. In other words, the people of the modern West, again, around the late 20th century, began to challenge the longstanding norm of having arranged/strategic marriages and instead decided that, as a culture, it would marry for love; and this remains the case today.

SIDENOTE

If it makes it easier, you can simply think of this cultural change as a specific behavioral drift influenced by a much broader societal shift that was brought on by the luxuries of first world life. Case in point, much like how we now eat for flavor, not just nutrition, we now marry for love, not just to bolster our social status, meet our political goals, and/or raise healthy children.

Now the reason it is important to note this cultural change is that this has subsequently altered our entire image of marriage in the modern West, and as a sane citizen I feel that the laws should account for this change. This is to say that if marriage is not explicitly about resources and/or function anymore, then what is it about, and what type of involvement should the government have. I.e., what do they stand to gain from being involved in the marriage business if we now marry exclusively for our feelings? Well, as I already suggested in the last paragraph, the answer to that first question is love, but when it comes to the second one, put plainly, to the government, who in all reality could care less about this change, marriage still has a very functional purpose. So, I suppose the real question, then, is what is that purpose, and is it ok for the government, in this day and age, to view marriage in that way.

To answer the first part of that question, put simply, marriage leads to more healthy, stable, and productive citizens being born. Now this probably seems like a no-brainer to many of you reading who lean more conservative in your political beliefs, but I will have you know that it is also a sentiment that researchers on the left agree with as well. For example, Child Trends, a left-leaning research organization focused on improving the lives of children and youth concluded in a report published on The Heritage Foundations website that,

> *Research clearly demonstrates that family structure matters for children, and the family structure that helps children the most is a family headed by two biological parents in a low-conflict marriage. Children in single-parent families, children born to unmarried mothers, and children in stepfamilies or cohabiting relationships face higher risks of poor outcomes... There is thus value for children in promoting strong, stable marriages between biological parents... It is not simply the presence of two parents, but the presence of two biological parents that seems to support children's development.*

Ok, so there is agreement on both sides of the political aisle, not just the right, that marriage makes better citizens, which is something that the government obviously want; but with that said, the government wants a lot of things, some of which they have no business wanting, such as a disarmed population and/or a population that doesn't value its privacy. So, despite the fact that marriage is something they should theoretically care about, should the government actually get what it wants when it comes to using this practice to produce better citizens; even when We the People no longer view it as something purely functional?

Well, I reckon that there are two ways to answer that last question, both of which are sane in their own way, but only one of which is realistic. Let me explain. The first way to answer that aforementioned question is that, since Westerners no longer view marriage as something centered around making new humans and/or moving up in the world, the government should actually not have anything to do with the practice at all. Now I am aware that this is a very stark Libertarian opinion, but nonetheless, it makes a lot of sense, especially to me because, in essence, this stance posits that it is a dangerous precedent for a government to try and incentivize our personal behavior. I mean, what if they wanted healthier adult citizens and therefore decided to ban restaurants? Is that the government's place to make sure we only eat their state-issued health rations? Of course not! So yeah, this position, though somewhat fringe, is quite logical. But be that as it may, I am not getting my hopes up for this answer because, as we all know, the government is generally not one to "uninvolve" itself once it is a part of something. Ergo, this is why I said that only one of these two ways of answering is actually realistic.

SIDENOTE

Because the Constitution does not make any mention of marriage, technically this first answer *is* the most Constitutionally sound one. Furthermore, if this is the correct answer, well, then our entire discussion on marriage, and same-sex marriage, essentially, ends there. I.e., if the government shouldn't be involved in marriage, then there is no need for a sane position because there shouldn't be any legislation to have a position on in the first place. Of course, with this said I didn't stop writing after giving this answer because, put plainly, I want you to know not only the best position, but also the best possible position. I.e., Our government quite often sticks its nose where it doesn't belong, but instead of simply throwing out the baby with the bathwater in these circumstances, I would rather you still try to find, at the very least, a sane position, even if it's not technically the right position. Anyway, still keep this first answer in the back of your mind as you continue to ponder this issue.

Alright, moving on, the second answer, which as I said we have been kind of forced to accept, for now anyway, is that it *is* okay for the government to do what it can to incentivize the production of good citizens. In other words, marriage is the government's business. Now, again, I do not like this answer, but since this is the realistic framework we exist under and the government is going to be involved in marriage whether we like it or not, at least for now (We the People can change this!), let's look at how they have been involved in the past, as well as what the law says about their current involvement. Then, if all goes well, we will be able to figure out what a sane and constitutionally sound position on same-sex marriage in particular should be, and if the current laws reflect that position.

SIDENOTE

Notice that this is also where the two sides of the aisle disagree. In other words, the crux of the debate is not whether marriage should be regulated, but rather *who* can get married. Ergo, technically neither side is against marriage as a practice, or against the government being involved in the ordeal. Rather, the friction point between the two sides of the aisle when it comes to marriage is pretty much centered solely around *who* can get married.

When it comes to the government's involvement in marriage, during my research I was surprised to find out that for a significant period of America's history the federal government actually had nothing to do with the affair at all. Instead, marriage was primarily regulated on a state-by-state basis. However, with that said, in 1913, for the first time in our history, this changed and marriage became formerly recognized in federal law with the passage of the Revenue Act of 1913. Now, I do have to mention that this act was mostly about tariffs and taxes, not marriage, but be that as it may, it did include new tax codes for married couples, thus making it the first-ever federal legislation to state that marriage is a legitimate and federally regulated institution. Ergo, even though it wasn't exclusively about marriage, it was still a rather important point in the history of federal marriage legislation. Of course, as with any new legislation, there were still quite a few gaps in this Act, legally speaking, such as what marriage actually meant in a legal sense, and if that definition applied to same-sex couples as well. In fact, pretty much the only marriage concern that the federal government had at the time was interracial marriage, and not much more.

An example of this concern is Democrat Congressman Seaborn Roddenberry of Georgia who, despite the fact that interracial marriage was pretty much universally banned by all of the states at that point, tried to pass a bill that would enforce a federal ban on the practice. And he wasn't shy about his convictions either. Now, he has many quotes that discuss his issues with interracial marriage, but one that I found to be particularly enlightening is as follows:

Intermarriage between whites and blacks is repulsive and averse to every sentiment of pure American spirit. It is abhorrent and repugnant. It is subversive to social peace.

Pretty intense, right? Well, fortunately, at least as far as individual liberty is concerned, Congressman Roddenberry's bill was shot down by the US legislature. This is to say that eventually interracial marriage was federally legalized in 1967 when the Supreme Court overturned a prior decision that allowed states to ban them if they so choose, and the court's thought process behind this decision was simple and is something you should be aware of moving forward. Basically, the thought process was that the fourteenth amendment, which grants equal rights to all citizens regardless of race or ethnicity, protects the practice of interracial marriage. But what about same-sex couples though?

Well, as fate would have it, up until 1967 the law had remained rather quiet on the same-sex aspect of the marriage debate. I suppose that this is partially due to same-sex couples being culturally shunned, and therefore not worthy of federal consideration, and also because marriage, at this point in time, was still mostly centered around procreation. Nonetheless, it didn't take long for homosexuals to get their time on the national debate stage, and in 1973 Maryland became the first state to formerly, and by statute I might add, recognize marriage as a union between a man and a woman. Then after this, much like how New York's 1955 "Abortion in America" conference started a cultural snowball effect that led to many other states expanding abortion rights, Conservatives rode the momentum wave created by Maryland's decision, and shortly thereafter many states decided to formally ban same-sex marriage themselves. However, despite this newfound interest in same-sex marriage by the state legislatures, the federal government still kept silent on the issue and the gaps in the Revenue Act of 1913 remained open.

SIDENOTE

There are a lot of interesting goings-on before 1913, such as women fighting for the right to not be considered property once in wedlock, and there are also a lot of interesting goings-on before and after 1973, such as Bill Clinton's 1996 Defense of Marriage Act that outlawed any federal recognition of same-sex and polyamorous marriages. For time's sake, though, we will not get into all of these because, frankly, I could write an entire book discussing them. So, with that said, the key takeaways of this section are that in 1913 marriage became a federally recognized and regulated practice, the main concern early on was interracial marriages which were made federally legal in 1967, and gay marriage was either not mentioned or banned on a state level during all of these periods but was not addressed at all on a federal level.

Continuing ever onward in our discussion of the federal government's involvement in marriage, despite all of the progressive post-1913 movements aimed at reforming federal laws regarding interracial marriages, same-sex couples have gotten very little attention from federal lawmakers, aside from Bill Clinton's 1996 Defense of Marriage Act that is. This, however, changed in the summer of 2015. To put it another way, essentially, on June 26th, 2015, the Supreme Court passed down its verdict on the contentious Obergefell v. Hodges case, a case that was centered around same-sex marriage rights, and as you have probably surmised, given that same-sex marriage is now legal, their decision was that the Fourteenth Amendment applies to same-sex couples just as it does to interracial couples. More than that, though, it also set the legal precedent that the right to marry was not just a matter of policy, but also that it should be considered a fundamental human right. Now this second part is interesting (and relevant) because the Constitution itself actually doesn't mention marriage at all. So, this precedent, though not explicitly grounded in the Constitution (Though you could make a case that it is since it stems from the Fourteenth Amendment.), does make the right to marry whomever you wish one of our inherent liberties, similar to freedom of speech, the right to bear arms, and every other constitutional right we possess. I digress though. At any rate, even though homosexuals, for the most part, were historically left out of the national marriage debate in the US, same-sex marriages, as of 2015, are now federally recognized and state governments are required by the federal government to view them the same as they would heterosexual marriages.

Ok, I know that we have covered a lot of information in a relatively short amount of time, but by now you should at least be familiar with what marriage is, why it became a human behavior (I.e., it has an evolutionary cause), the personal benefits associated with it, why the government cares about marriage, and also a little bit about its legal history in the US. Furthermore, you should also understand when and why gay marriage was legalized, as well as how recent of a decision this was, which, as a sidenote, helps explain why it is still such a hot-button issue to many people. All good and ready to move on? Awesome, because despite all of the information I just threw at you, we still have one more thing to do before closing out this chapter. That is, we still have to figure out what a sane position is in regard to same-sex marriage today, and if the current laws reflect that sane position.

SIDENOTE

Again, there is a sane argument to be made when it comes to the government not being involved in the practice of marriage at all, and I would wager this is actually the sanest of the arguments, but this is also a pipe dream at the moment. So, let's just assume the government will be involved whilst establishing our sane position. Now if that annoys you and you are sitting there wishing I would just stick to my laurels and focus on the non-involvement argument, well, welcome to my world wherein individual liberty is king. Put frankly, it is lonely here, and quite often frustrating because We the People, broadly speaking are generally rather lazy when it comes to politics. In other words, the reason we have to "work with what we got," much to our Libertarian chagrin, is because the active citizenry has thus far allowed the federal government to get involved in things it has no business being in without any consequences. Make sense? Ok, Libertarian-style rant over. In sum, if you don't like the government being involved in marriage, help me get the culture on our side so that We the People can get the government to butt out of the affair.

So, what is a sane position on same-sex marriage. To begin, the main sticking point for me when I first started to think about the legalization of gay marriage was that, in an evolutionary sense, it goes against nature, and therefore legalizing it does not serve any purpose that the government should theoretically respect, such as making stable and healthy citizens, for instance. Now when I say that I do not want it to be misconstrued and for me to be seen as a Bible thumper who believes homosexuals are an abomination (Again, I want the government out of marriage. This is just figuring out how they should be involved if I can't get them out.), so let me clarify. As previously stated, essentially, our main purpose for existing is to pass on our genes, at least from a scientific perspective. And in addition to this, single-mate monogamous pair bonds (marriages) are a very good way of ensuring this process has the highest chance of succeeding. Therefore, marriage, in all its many culturally specific forms, is an evolutionarily inspired and beneficial behavior. Furthermore, our government, an extension of evolutionarily developed human behavior (at least according to Aristotle, "Man is by nature a political animal"), has recognized all of this, as well as marriage's societal benefits for over 100 years. Thus it makes sense why they decided to codify its significance into law circa 1913. Gay marriage, though, is not an evolutionarily beneficial behavior. This is to say that, in essence, it is a quirk in our evolution and this should make the government, who has historically viewed marriage as a means for producing good citizens, see it as inherently different than heterosexual marriage because it does not serve the same societal purpose that those types of marriages do/did. Ergo, when I initially began to think about this issue my sticking point was, pretty much, if the government is involved, what is the point of the government legalizing same-sex marriage if this means that they are giving up all of the benefits (tax incentives/breaks, etc.) without getting any of the rewards (new, healthy, and stable citizens).

Well, with all of that said, eventually my sticking point was…. unstuck? Whatever, the point is, when I began to think about how our cultural views of marriage have changed post-20th century it began to make more sense why the federal government would reevaluate gay marriage. In other words, I now recognize that **a)** the reason marriage exists has changed within the West (we now marry for love, not other more practical reasons), and **b)** since our reasons for getting married have changed, if the government is to be involved in the ordeal it should also view it in this way as well, not it in the old way wherein marriages were instituted for a practical and functional societal purpose.

SIDENOTE

An important addendum, especially after talking about why the government actually cares about marriage in the first place, is that the Constitution never promised us the *best* society, only the freest society. So, using the "It's what's best for society" rationale to make laws is not an acceptable thing for the federal government to do. As I said, if it was…. well, you should get ready to say goodbye to Burger King and hello to government health rations.

Therefore, with all of that said, my conclusion as to what a sane position is in regard to the issue of same-sex marriage is that if the government *is* going to be involved in marriage, and they do not require couples, including heterosexual couples, to provide a societally beneficial justification to get married, such as plans to procreate or further historical family bloodlines, for instance, and are instead ok with people getting married for no other reason than love; well, then they cannot state that certain marriages, though a bit quirky (from an evolutionary perspective), are invalid simply because their *only* foundation is love, not function. Ergo, the sane citizen's position on same-sex marriage should be that if the government is, in fact, involved in the institution of marriage (again, I'd prefer not), then it must allow all of its citizens to engage in the practice equally. In other words, if the government wants to incentivize marriages because they are good for society while also allowing people to marry solely for love, then they must forgo the privilege of treating marriage as a purely business-like and functional endeavor. And this means that they must take the proverbial crunchy with the smooth in so far as they must also accept the fact that, in a free society, when you allow societally beneficial marriages (heterosexual marriages) to exist based solely on love, some non-societally beneficial marriages (same-sex marriages) based solely on love will exist as well.

SIDENOTE

Like I said at the end of the last chapter, I imagine many of you will still disagree with this sane position. That's ok. I mean, coming from a very religious background myself, I understand better than most the reality that marriage can and does mean very different things to people depending on their personal cultures and/or religions. Hell, this is why I am not a fan of government involvement in the first place. However, with that said, to those who disagree with my position because of a personal reason, such as religion, and not a Constitutional and/or legal one, ask yourself this. Which scenario, if the government *is* involved, would you rather have? A country wherein all citizens are allowed to marry whomever they wish for no other reason than love, or a country wherein the government has specific guidelines for those that wish to marry. Just food for thought because, as we have seen countless times throughout history, once you give the government the power to discriminate against people, it generally does. And worse than that, generally We the People have very little control over who gets discriminated against once that precedent has been set. I.e., Maybe at first it is just the same-sex couples that get restricted, but how long until it is Republicans, Democrats, or even religious people who are discriminated against? Case in point, you are only ever one leader away from the government changing its mind and making you the problem.

Alright, that's it for this one folks. In closing, as we discussed in the last chapter the government cannot make laws based on religion, therefore, the only logical legal objection that I see to legalizing gay marriage is that it does not perform the same societal function as heterosexual marriage. Well, if that sounds about right and you want this to be the way the government views same-sex marriage, as something that it must regulate to make society better that is, just remember that you would be setting the stage for the government to start legislating marriage in whatever way it feels would best serve society's needs. Sure, maybe that means that religious conservatives would get their way for a while, but how long until power shifted the other way and openly religious people were actually the ones not allowed to get married because the government decided that, instead of *good* citizens, they raise fanatics? I don't know about you, but when I think about what those types of futures could look like I am forced to deem anyone who would support laying the foundation for them insane. In other words, like Thomas Jefferson, I sanely choose the consequences of too much liberty over the consequences of not enough liberty. Anyway, see you all in the next chapter wherein we be discussing a very divisive issue known as transgenderism.

CHAPTER 5

Transgenderism

America. What a weird country, am I right? I mean, we have all kinds of people here doing all kinds of wild stuff, and full disclosure, I'd say this is a good thing. However, one of the symptoms of having as much liberty as we have here in America is that some people end up going, to put it lightly, a little nuts. Now, to each their own because the last thing I want is the government dictating what a *good* way to live is for its citizens, but when it comes to the government legislating legitimate state power, there does need to be at least a small tether to reality; and this is why I approached abortion and same-sex marriage the way I did, from a logical, constitutional, and scientific position, and also why I will now be addressing our next topic, transgenderism, in the same fashion. This is to say that I believe in individual liberty and We the People's power over the nation-state above all else, but when it comes to this highly divisive issue I do think that a bit of sane legislation is needed because, unlike something like same-sex marriage, for instance, wherein the government actually has no legitimate reason to be involved, transgenderism is an issue that transcends the walls of the citizenry's private bedrooms, and therefore is, in essence, an issue that concerns all of us. What I mean by this is that transgenderism in particular is an issue that has a quite a few significant impacts on the US population as a whole, and some of these impacts, such as the ones it has on underage children and female-only spaces are ones that force sane citizens to raise questions about how We the People can best support the ideal of individual liberty, while also protecting the constitutional rights of America's most vulnerable citizens (which is one of the few legitimate roles of our government). Alright, so now that you have an idea as to why I decided to discuss transgenderism in this book, let's begin by talking about what it actually is, and if it's new.

SIDENOTE

This chapter turned out to be longer than I expected, but when I started, I thought it would be short. Well, even though this one wasn't, quite frankly, some of these issues are pretty cut and dry. So, I just wanted to let you know here and now that instead of trying to needlessly stretch out every chapter to "normal" length, I figure with some of them I will just say what needs to be said and leave it at that, regardless of how long, or rather not long that makes said chapter. Anyway, let's get back to this "normal" length chapter and find a sane position on this issue. Sound good?

Put plainly, a transgender person is a person whose gender deviates from their biological sex. Now this definition will face rejection from people on the right side of the aisle, and even some on the left, because most people, for all of human history, have only recognized two sexes. The issue with this criticism, though, (don't get too excited pro-trans readers) is that, technically, this definition is correct because gender does not actually mean the same thing as sex despite the fact that both are often and incorrectly used interchangeably. Ergo, if we are to truly understand what *transgender* is, I suppose the first thing that we need to do is figure out what gender actually is, since everyone, for the most part, already knows what sex is (male or female).

Alright, so what is gender. To begin, before 1945 gender was simply a grammatical term for sex. This is to say that, pre-WWII, essentially, sex and gender were defined to mean the same thing. However, in 1945 this longstanding status quo changed when Dr. Madison Bentley challenged this norm and redefined the term gender to instead mean the "socialized obverse of sex," thus making him the first person in the West to see gender as something fundamentally different from sex; and in the academic community, this move was groundbreaking. But be this as it may, for the most part this new concept was primarily confined to high academia and didn't really gain traction among the populace until 1955 when sexologist John Money used the term in a scientific journal wherein he not only used the new term, but also expanded Dr. Bentley's definition stating that gender is "all those things that a person says or does to disclose himself or herself as having the status of boy or man, girl or woman." In other words, John believed that gender is something that is similar to and even draws inspiration from the male/female sex dichotomy, but is also something that is inherently different because instead of having its roots in biology, gender has to do with how someone interacts with their environment. Ergo, to John Money a transgender person is a person who, regardless of their biological sex, feels that their internal feelings and/or external behaviors do not align with that biology. I.e., think about a skinny person who feels as if they are very fat. Yes, that person may be very tiny, but if they wear a fat suit and buy two seats on an airplane then, even though they are biologically skinny, their identity and behaviors are nonetheless those of a fat person. Make sense?

SIDENOTE

For the pro-trans folks out there, note that I am excluding going into the biological arguments surrounding multiple sexes. Let me explain why I made that decision. Yes, there are people born with unique chromosomal patterns that deviate from the traditional XY (male) or XX (female) dichotomy and some examples of these are X, XXY, XXXY, and XYY; but to be frank, these abnormalities simply do not constitute additional sexes. Instead, they are genetic anomalies, much like Down Syndrome (a person born with an extra copy of chromosome 21) or Klinefelter syndrome (a male born with an extra X chromosome). Therefore, much like a person born with no legs is not a new species, people with these "evolutionary defects" are not members of a new sex. Rather, they are males and females who simply have a diagnosable and often detrimental genetic disorder.

Now to be very honest, as someone who has a graduate degree in the social sciences, as well as quite a bit of empirical research experience, all of this gender stuff seems a bit frivolous. I mean, I think that people should be allowed to express themselves in any way they please, but gender, it appears to me, can just be summed up as an aspect of personality. With that said, though, if we are to find a sane position on transgenderism, we must fully understand the worldview that gender theorists are operating from. That is why it is important to thoroughly understand what the term gender means, and therefore why I detailed its technical definition. In other words, whether you "believe" in gender or not, you still need to know what it actually is.

Okay, moving on. In essence, gender is a non-biological aspect of who a person is that is modeled from the inherent male/female dichotomy of biological sex, and understanding this can actually help put into perspective where the two sides of the aisle disagree. This is to say that the left tends to treat gender as, essentially, a second sex that oftentimes takes priority over biological sex, and the right tends to look at gender as something that the left is trying to replace biological sex with, at least in instances of transgender people that is. Sound familiar? Well, in all reality both of these are wrong because, according to the technical definition, gender, regardless of whether you believe it is a legitimate theory or not, is a concept having to do with how one personally sees themselves within the male/female continuum and not something tied to their biological sex. Ergo, at the end of the day it is fair to say that, broadly speaking, neither side of the political aisle really disagrees all that much with the male/female sex dichotomy, but they do, however, disagree about the validity and/ or importance of the very separate concept of gender. In lay terms, gender is the point of disagreement, not sex.

SIDENOTE

The pro-trans readers/listeners are probably a bit jilted that, in addition to not addressing the biological arguments for multiple sexes, I also did not cover the history of transgenderism, well, before 1945 that is. At any rate, the reason for this is simple. This is to say that, yes, there is an argument to be made that many cultures throughout history have recognized multiple genders

(Hijra, Calalai, Calabai, Bissu, Muxe, etc.), however, these cultural beliefs aren't really relevant to transgenderism today. I mean, there are many cultures that used to believe that the earth was flat as well, but I could not use these cultural beliefs as evidence of a flat earth today because, put plainly, we now have enough empirical scientific evidence that these beliefs are, essentially, irrelevant/outdated in regard to that debate. Ergo, since we live in a time where medicine and science are more advanced than ever, I simply do not feel the need to incorporate subjective and/or anecdotal information from ancient cultures that would, essentially, do nothing to further our scientific understanding of transgenderism. So, to the pro-trans readers/listeners, just know that I am not intentionally being unfair to your side, I am simply being scientifically sound and following the evidence.

Ok, since we have now parsed out that gender is different from sex, and also that I just see it as an aspect of one's personality, I don't feel that any more time is needed when it comes to discussing the definition of transgenderism. Frankly, you now know what it is and you either believe that gender theory, and transgenderism by proxy, is relevant or you don't. Either way I want to keep moving so that we can get to the far more important part of this chapter, the legislative questions surrounding transgenderism. Good to go?

To begin, as it stands now transgender legislation is primarily taking place on the state level. In fact, the only real movement on the federal side of things has been adding transgenders and other LGBTQ+ people to already existing legislation, like the Fourteenth Amendment, which we discussed in the last chapter. With that said, though, this issue is rather new, and also not clearly and/or explicitly mentioned in the Constitution, so I imagine it won't be long until we do see federal legislation coming down the pipe for it. Well, because of this likely soon to come federal intervention, and because we, the sane citizens, have to be ready no matter what level of government we are dealing with, I am going to forgo getting into the endless list of state-level laws and will instead focus on transgenderism more broadly so that, much like with abortion, you will have a sane position on the issue no matter where you are.

So when it comes to the transgenderism debate as a whole, in my summation there are three main areas where political friction is occurring. These are gender-specific places (bathrooms, spas, etc.), sports (Fallon Fox and other biological males competing in female sports), and children (Hormone blockers and irreversible gender-reaffirming surgeries). Starting with gender-specific places, a recent example of this friction is the controversy surrounding Wi Spa in California. To explain, in essence this controversy occurred because Wi Spa allowed trans women to use their female locker room. Well, as you can imagine this did not sit well with many of the biological women at the spa, especially after the 52-year-old male-to-female transgender individual in question reportedly began walking around the locker room with their male genitalia out and fully exposed, and soon the incident became a national news story that once again reignited the trans bathroom debate among the American populace.

Now when it comes to this particular situation, from a legal standpoint what is interesting is that, even though the 52-year-old offender was charged with five counts of indecent exposure, many people, including the staff of Wi Spa itself, are making the counter-argument that they were actually the ones following the law, not the cops. In other words, the argument for this side of the debate is that, due to the preexisting equal opportunity laws, they actually had no choice but to let the transgender individual use the female locker room because, if they had stopped him then they would be, essentially, discriminating against a trans woman based solely on their gender identity, which, technically speaking, is illegal. Now I won't lie to you, I am not a legal expert, but I do have to say that this argument is a rather intriguing one, but then again, so is the other one. So, who is right? In other words, should the trans woman have been allowed to use the women's locker room, or should women's spaces be reserved solely for biological women?

Well, as I said earlier, there is actually no mention of transgenderism in the constitution; however, with that said I do believe that there is a sane solution to conundrums like the one Wi Spa had to face. This is to say that the reason we established female-only spaces in the first place is that men and women are inherently different and the chances of men physically abusing women are much higher than those of women physically abusing men. I.e., in general men are, put bluntly, stronger, faster, and/or hornier than women. Ergo, to protect women's inherent constitutional right to engage in life, liberty, and the pursuit of happiness, we, as a society, have decided to give them private spaces where men cannot prey on them at their most vulnerable.

Now I don't know about you, but I think that most of us here in America can agree that this is a sane thing to do. Therefore, I believe that it is quite reasonable to belief that biological women simply should not have to be subjected to the threat of male predation simply because some people feel that their gender takes precedence over their sex. In other words, the sane solution/position in regard to this aspect of the transgenderism debate is that women's only spaces should, in fact, be spaces that do not inherently contain the threat of possible male predation, no matter how rare, because this fear of predation clearly inhibits their right to engage in life, liberty, and the pursuit of happiness. Make sense?

SIDENOTE

It is worth noting that there is a somewhat self-correcting aspect to this bathroom debate. What I mean by this is that, if a trans person is not identifiable, AKA they clearly pass for the opposite sex, then this whole thing is not an issue. In other words, if you look like a woman, then no one will notice and/or care that you are using a woman's only space. However, if you have a 5'oclock shadow and your twig and berries are out on full display, well, then the situation changes a bit, doesn't it? Anyway, this is all to say that it appears to me the trans community could avoid this issue becoming a national concern in the first place if they would simply meet the anti-trans community halfway and stop calling everyone a bigot who doesn't want a dude with a beard showering with their wife and daughters. I don't know, maybe I am just too old fashioned for this modern world.

Ok, so the second area where the transgenderism debate is experiencing friction is sports. More specifically, it appears to me that the friction is centered around male-to-female trans athletes competing in and dominating sporting competitions designated exclusively for women. Now I actually wrote an article on this subject that, unfortunately, is yet to be published, but nonetheless I wanted to share it here in lieu of "re-explaining" my sane position on this issue because I feel that it succinctly sums up what a sane position is in regard to this aspect of the transgenderism debate in an easy to understand way.

(Perhaps this is cheating, but I already wrote the article, so I just look at it as being economical with my writing session. Anyway, see you on the flip side.)

Chess, Trans Athletes, and the Free Market
"The International Chess Federation just showed
the world how to handle transgender athletes"

Transgender athletes are becoming increasingly more common in athletic competitions and this has spurred a great deal of criticism from the right side of the political aisle. Their argument is simple. Men have a distinct advantage when it comes to sports.

This point seems self-evident given the immense amount of success most trans athletes (typically male to female) experience when they decide to change gender. CeCe Telfer, Mary Gregory, and Rachel McKinnon are a few examples of this in that they were all mediocre male athletes who are now, put frankly, dominating in their respective fields, and setting world records in hurdling, weightlifting, and cycling.

Despite the seemingly obvious biological benefits that come with being a male athlete, many on the left side of the aisle still deny there is a relevant difference. In an audio interview conducted by NPR, host Scott Detrow spoke with established geneticist Dr. Eric Vilain who believes that there simply isn't enough evidence to suggest that men have a disproportionate competitive advantage in sports.

"Well, on one hand, not having an indiscriminate ban suggests that the baseline for eligibility for all athletes, including trans athletes, should be inclusion. And I think that's a good thing.

And that's actually what the International Olympic Committee has done in creating a framework for inclusion and fairness that's based on the principle of no presumption of advantage. And if a category is going to be excluded, it needs to be based on evidence. The problem here with the exclusion on a case-by-case basis is that it is likely not to be based on evidence. Who's going to undertake all the necessary research to demonstrate a disproportionate advantage, sport by sport, at so many different ages? Who will fund this? Likely not the school systems."

"The issue is we lack a lot of data, so we, in fact, know very little about advantages of trans girls and women athletes over their cisgender peers. That's true in elite competitions. That's true in school sports."

"I'll end by saying that the larger question really goes beyond a simple competitive advantage. It's whether there is a disproportionate competitive advantage between trans and cis athletes."

Aside from pushing a partisan narrative or reinforcing the party line, there is no good reason why Dr. Vilain, an accomplished geneticist, would say these things. The reason for this is that science has, in fact, provided quite a bit of evidence regarding the advantage male athletes have over their female counterparts.

What the research has shown is that men have a clear advantage when it comes to sports. For starters, men have larger and denser bones, which leads to an increased ability to support muscle mass, as well as an increased mechanical advantage, thus increasing their ability to perform tasks that require strength, speed, and power. Furthermore, men have a much higher VO2 max threshold. In other words, due to biological males having larger hearts than biological females, men's bodies are much better when it comes to delivering oxygen to their muscles and tissues during exercise.

Now the reason these two *disproportionate* advantages are important to note is that neither has to do explicitly with testosterone, which is the typical go-to argument of anti-trans activists. This is to say that, unlike testosterone, which can be increased or decreased via artificial means, bone density, and heart size are not parts of the body that doctors can alter. In other words, they are clear-cut cut, and more importantly, unchangeable advantages that no amount of gender-confirming care can eliminate.

As this evidence shows, it is not fair for biological males to compete in female sports. With that said, however, more and more male-to-female transgender athletes seem to be making the decision to switch proverbial teams. In some states, this is being heralded as brave and heroic while in others it is leading to serious legislative crackdowns. So, what is the proper way to handle trans athletes while pleasing both sides?

Despite chess being a sport that no one really thinks about while discussing trans athletes, The International Chess Federation (FIDE) has recently found itself at the center of the debate by making the decision to "effectively stop allowing transgender women from participating in women's competitions until 'further analysis' can be made."

This decision, though from an unlikely source, may have actually exposed an answer to this debate that will make all of this trans athlete stuff, effectively, a non-issue. The reason for this is that chess has a unique aspect that most sports do not share. This aspect is an "open" section, which is a category in tournaments that allows both men and women to compete against each other.

Per FIDE's decision, trans chess players will still be allowed to compete in these open sections, thus allowing them to continue competing despite their decision to transition.

Could this be the answer America has been looking for? Think about it.

People on the left argue that trans people are far more common than the average person realizes. More specifically, they say that the research suggests that 1.3-5% of the US population identifies as a gender different from the one they were assigned at birth and that this number is likely higher, but due to under-reporting those people are still not being accounted for.

Of course, people on the right have and will continue to deny these statistics/assumptions, but they don't want trans athletes competing anyway, so as far as the left is concerned, who cares, right?

Assuming that this argument is valid and there truly are this many trans people out there in the populace, well, when it comes to sports, why not just create open leagues? Wouldn't this give those on the right what they want, biological men and women competing with biological men and women, and wouldn't it also give the left what they want, a safe and inclusive place for trans athletes to compete?

The answer as to why we do not have open leagues is probably that there are not actually enough trans people to fill the ranks of these divisions, though the left will never admit it. But to be honest, this is an irrelevant and unconstitutional criticism of open leagues. You see, at the end of the day the Constitution is all about protecting individual rights and free market principles. This, among other things, means protecting the right of women, who are disproportionately affected by trans athletes, to have fair and safe spaces. In addition to this, a free market, which is what made America what it is today, operates via supply and demand. Therefore, if there are not enough trans athletes to support open sports leagues, well, then that is just, unfortunately, the way it is and you don't get to infringe upon women's rights to remedy this.

In closing, sports are all about meritocracy. In a way, they are a perfect example of how a free market should work. This is to say that sports are driven by a supply of talented athletes who meet the demands of the population's viewing preferences. Because of this, sports are highly competitive. This is why you don't see 5'2 people competing in the NBA or overweight people competing in the 100-meter dash. So, if the integrity of sports is to be upheld while also protecting women's constitutional rights, which would mean not allowing athletes who are born male to use their inherent biological advantages against athletes who were born female, the only logical solution is to leave things up to the free market by making a separate place for trans athletes to freely compete against one another. If you think this isn't a feasible idea, well, chess did it.......

As this article explains, biological men have distinct and inherent advantages when it comes to strength, speed, and endurance. Furthermore, it discusses how many of these advantages cannot be reduced via hormone treatments. Ergo, there is a very clear reason why female sports should be protected. In other words, it is sane to protect women's sports not only because of safety concerns (look up Fallon Fox, a male-to-female transgender MMA fighter beating the crap out of biological women), but also because having these safe outlets for female athletes to compete protects these women's opportunities from being unfairly taken away by biological men. Of course, with that said, I do still believe that sports organizations should be allowed to do whatever they want in regard to allowing trans women to compete against biological women; however, my point more broadly is simply that the sane position in regard to this aspect of the debate is that, just like sports organizations should be allowed to harbor trans athletes, so too should sports organizations be allowed to bar non-biological females from competing. In other words, because it is sane and constitutionally permitted to protect women's rights, and because this would not infringe upon transgender people's constitutional rights due to the fact that they can still compete in other places (I.e., leagues designated for their biological sex and/or open leagues), the decision about how to handle this decision should be left up to the organizations themselves and not the federal government, and this applies regardless of whether or not the government is providing them financial support I might add. (FYI, this "let the organizations choose" stance also applies to female-only spaces, by the way. I.e., let businesses do what they want and allow *them* to be the ones to decide if they want to open their female-only spaces to biological males. Capeesh?)

SIDENOTE

In regard to this next section, all of the studies I looked at regarding hormone blockers and desistance rates among transgender youth are available in the references section. So, if you do not want to take me at my word, please feel free to look them up yourself. In fact, I encourage you to do this.

Moving on, the third and arguably most heated dimension of the transgender debate involves providing hormone blockers and irreversible gender-affirming surgeries to underage children. Now to be honest, since this dimension of the debate involves a lot of science it is actually far less ambiguous than the former two. In other words, it is pretty clear cut, at least as far as a sane citizen is concerned. With that said, though, I would still like to briefly cover it.

To begin, when it comes to hormone blockers, which are drugs used to postpone puberty among adolescents, put frankly, the argument that they are reversible is a fallacy, and this is agreed upon even by trans-friendly institutions, like the Mayo Clinic, for instance, who recently stated that (2023), "though puberty can be resumed after hormone blockers are ceased, long-term effects such as decreased bone density, stunted bone growth, and infertility are still common." And in addition to this, a 56-page UK study entitled *Short-term outcomes of pubertal suppression in a selected cohort of 12 to 15-year-old young people with persistent gender dysphoria in the UK* by Carmichael et al., stated that alongside these long-term negative physical symptoms researchers also noticed no improvement in the youth's psychological well-being after undergoing their respective hormone therapies. To put that another way, negative consequences aside, there really weren't any negligible positive consequences of adolescents suffering from gender dysphoria using hormone therapy either.

Now, there are many more studies that back this information up (again, see the references section), but for time's sake, I will not get into all of those here. So, if you are short on memory space, just remember that hormone blockers are not reversible, at least not completely, and that they do come with negative long-term physical effects. Furthermore, according to the research, they also do not significantly improve the psychological distress that adolescents experience while going through a gender crisis. Ergo, the juice, most certainly, is not worth the squeeze, and the practice is therefore, in my summation, insane.

Alright, pushing ever onward, when it comes to finding a sane position on this third part of the transgenderism debate, transgender children that is, in lay terms, gender reassignment/gender-affirming surgeries do not require as much explanation to understand as hormone blockers do because, put simply, it is obvious that these procedures are not reversible. With that said, though, we still need to figure out if they have long-term negative impacts, both physically and psychologically, if we are to really determine if they are sane or not. So, because this is still an important part of the transgenderism debate, despite the answer being somewhat self-evident, let's get into it and wrap this thing up.

Alright, so when it comes to gender affirming care, also referred to as gender reassignment surgery, the unfortunate news for pro-trans activists is that these procedures, on top of being irreversible, do in fact also carry with them a somewhat high probability of negative consequences, at least as far as cosmetic procedures go, and these consequences can range all the way from mild permanent swelling of the genital area all the way to severe and recurrent infections caused by the human body trying to, essentially, heal the regions that were surgically altered. Of course, there is sort of a silver lining, though, in that severe issues like the latter one I mentioned happen in less than 10% of patients, but nonetheless, it is not unreasonable to say that, in the long-term, there is a significant degree of risk that comes with these procedures. Simple enough, right? Well, when it comes to the long-term psychological impacts of these procedures, things get a little bit more complicated. This is to say that, yes, the research shows that over 50% of adults who receive gender reassignment surgery do report it as having a positive impact on their mental health, however, with that said, another notable statistical reality is that 61-98% of adolescents, essentially, outgrow their gender crisis. In other words, at the low end, nearly two-thirds of children who identify as transgender will return to a gender that aligns with their biological sex by the time they become teenagers. So, is it really sane to justify allowing a child to take a step as dramatic and irreversible as gender reassignment surgery if most kids will simply return to their original gender without it? Or, given the high rates of physical consequences, is it better to forgo this extreme procedure?

Well, I suppose the answer to that last question is up to you guys, but for me, after reviewing all of this information, put plainly, it seems like the proverbial juice garnered from gender-affirming care for minors, be it hormone treatments or more permanent options such as surgery, just does not appear to be worth the metaphorical juice. I.e., given the high desistance rates among children who identify as transgender, highly invasive, and possibly damaging medical solutions do not seem like the sane way to go. Rather, it seems like a better solution is to simply wait for the children to become adults. Of course, with this said, there is another aspect of this debate that we must consider as well. That is, who gets to make this decision in the first place? In other words, is the government's job to force parents to make sane decisions in regard to their children, or is the ball in the parent's court when it comes to this issue?

SIDENOTE

To those who are concerned about the "trauma" going through puberty causes for a youth having a gender crisis, again, at the low end two thirds of them desist. Ergo, juice and squeeze.

Now to be honest, when it comes to who has the authority to make these decisions, I am extremely conflicted. This is to say that, on the one hand I rather dislike the notion of the government stepping in and telling parents how to raise their children. However, on the other hand, I think that it is one of the government's few legitimate roles to prevent actual child abuse. But the problem with that, though, is that there is no clear answer as to where to draw the line on child abuse. You see, I believe that it is insane for parents to allow their children to go on hormone blockers and/or undergo gender reassignment surgery; but I also can see, let's say in twenty years, the government classifying religious fundamentalists as extremists, and therefore *their* style of parenting as insane. For example, and this is one I have personally witnessed, what if in twenty years a child is treated by a psychiatrist because the fear of going to hell is literally giving them panic attacks? Is this child abuse? Well, depends on who you ask.

With all of that in mind, perhaps the closest I can get to a definitive answer in this matter is that it should remain, as it is now, at the state level. The reason for this is that unlike something that is clear cut, like abortion (I.e., when does life begin), for instance, when it comes to gender-affirming care for children the scientific community is still embroiled in controversy. Therefore, I must chalk this aspect of the transgenderism debate up to one of those aforementioned consequences of "too much liberty." This is to say that I would rather have some states allow parents to approve gender-affirming care for their children, even though it is likely unnecessary and will likely have adverse long-term effects, than have a federal government determining where the child abuse line is, at least when it comes to an issue as new and/or murky as this one. Of course, be that as it may, though, I am also open to the idea of We the People determining that gender-affirming care for minors is, in fact, child abuse, but only with the caveat that this decision comes with a widespread cultural recognition that We the People must be especially vigilant so that the government does not use this decision to propagate any future incursions upon parental rights. Good to go?

SIDENOTE

I do need to say, if for no other reason than my own sanity, that I believe the government should stop explicit and self-evident child abuse. I mean, the scientific community is not confused about the fact that a parent should not give their baby a tattoo or put cigarettes out on them. However, given how new transgenderism is, and especially in regard to children, I just don't know that it is clear-cut child abuse yet. At least not to the degree that it warrants allowing the federal government to get involved. Again, I know I sound like a broken record, but I am always cognizant of the fact that, when they can, the federal government will abuse its power. Anyway, now that I have made sure everyone knows I am anti-child abuse, let's move on.

Well folks, that is the end of the chapter. Just so that things are clear before we close this out, gender, as a concept, technically speaking is inherently different from sex, and this is true whether you personally accept the existence and/or validity of gender or not. Furthermore, the transgender debate as a whole really consists of three separate aspects. These are female-only spaces, sports, and children, and a sane position on the first two is that it is completely and constitutionally acceptable for an institution and/or organization to designate spaces exclusively for biological females; however, it is also completely and constitutionally acceptable for an institution to forgo this practice. Ergo, the government should let the free market handle these areas and should not intervene. Now when it comes to the third aspect, put plainly, it is insane to allow children to physically transition, however, it is also insane to have the federal government legislate this without understanding what this could open the door to. So, a sane position on this third aspect is that We the People must decide if we want the federal government to stop this insane behavior, and I think we should mind you, but if we do we must also become ever more vigilant in our defense of liberty and the fight against tyrannical government overreach. Alright, that's it folks. I'll see you all in the next chapter wherein we will be discussing environmentalism.

CHAPTER 6

Environmentalism

Alright, the next divisive issue that we are going to discuss in this book is one that, despite being a non-factor for most of America's history, has in recent years begun to experience a massive resurgence on the national debate stage, and is now something that prospective political candidates and elected leaders from both parties are being forced to address. Furthermore, this issue is quickly becoming one of if not *the* top political talking points among young voters, a critical demographic of the active citizenry that grows more and more outspoken and/or powerful every year I might add. Anyway, the issue I am referring to is environmentalism.

Now when it comes to environmentalism, I imagine those of you reading this who were adults in the 1970s can still remember when this issue first became a big deal in the US; but for those who weren't alive during this period of novel environmentalist hysteria, back then the major fear, which was spurred on by outlets such as Time magazine who in 1974 published a story entitled "Another Ice Age?" was that man-made climate change in the form of global cooling was, essentially, driving us into an extinction level environmental catastrophe. Well, as you may have noticed this is no longer a concern for environmentalists, and instead the new concern is quite literally the opposite of an ice age. That is to say that, as it stands currently global *cooling* has become a thing of the past and in its absence global *warming* has now become the primary concern of environmentalists. Interesting, aye?

At any rate, if you are a curious citizen like me, doesn't this relatively rapid 180° shift by the environmentalists make you wonder what changed? I mean, something drastic and obvious *must* have happened to cause this total reversal when it comes to what our planet's greatest environmental threat is, right? Well, unfortunately, it isn't as simple as all of that. You see, even though there are now far more "expert" opinions on this topic than there were in the 1970s, one could argue that (in part due to political tribalism) there are now also far more disagreements among these "experts." Ergo, finding reliable information on environmentalism and establishing how much of a threat it is in our current day and age can be a little tricky. So, since this is the case and the environmentalist science over the last 50 years seems to be, at the very least, a little inconsistent, we are going to have to dig for that answer in this chapter. In other words, in order to find a sane position on environmentalism in this chapter we are going to, in no specific order, pin down a firm definition of what environmentalism actually is, discuss whether or not it is a new concept, parse through what the most up-to-date science has to say about environmentalism, determine what the government's role should be in regard to this issue, and then we will review how the US Constitution factors into all of this. Then, after all of that, we are going to use this information to establish what a sane citizen's position should be when it comes to this confusing/divisive issue. Sound good?

SIDENOTE

The reason we are starting at square one with environmentalism (I.e., what is environmentalism), is that answering "what environmentalism actually is and what it aims to do" first will help us determine if this is even something that warrants a sane citizens' time to begin with. Furthermore, answering these questions is important because the main friction point between the two sides of the political aisle when it comes to this issue seems to be centered around answering the question, "Is the problem that environmentalism strives to solve a real problem." What I mean by this is that, in other words, the right side of the aisle, broadly speaking, denies that man-made climate change exists in the first place, which subsequently would mean that any environmentalist efforts are, essentially, pointless. Meanwhile, however, the left side of the aisle, again, broadly speaking, disagrees with this sentiment and instead sees climate change as an inherent and immediate threat, which obviously means that they subsequently view environmentalism as a worthwhile and necessary cause. Ergo, because the two sides seem to disagree on whether or not environmentalism serves a real purpose, if we are to find a sane position on it we must first figure out what its purported purpose truly is, and this involves, as we did with gender in the last chapter, first understanding the term in a technical sense. Good to go? Sweet.

Alright, at the outset I think that the best course of action for us to take is to figure out what environmentalism actually means. Well, according to Ole Reliable, which is what I have come to know

Webster's Dictionary as over the last several months, environmentalism can be defined in two different ways, which are as follows:

1. A theory that views environment rather than heredity as the important factor in the development and especially the cultural and intellectual development of an individual or group.

2. Advocacy of the preservation, restoration, or improvement of the natural environment

Now when it comes to these definitions, though similar, I actually see the first one as inherently different from the second one in that the first one, it appears, specifically refers to what I am now calling an environmentalist worldview, not necessarily environmentalism. What I mean by this is that, in essence, this first definition describes the mindset of a person who is looking beyond their own desires to advance themselves or their specific in-group (heredity) and instead sees the advancement of Earth as a whole (the environment) as a more just goal. In other words, it describes the mindset of a person who is more focused on *everything* around them as opposed to simply being concerned with themself.

The second definition, on the other hand, refers to how this environmentalist worldview is practically applied. This is to say that, if you are concerned with everything around you, and not just your own advancement (be it passing on your genes, meeting your own personal objectives, furthering your own bloodline/legacy, etc.) then you are going to advocate for, as the definition states, the preservation, restoration, or improvement of the natural environment. In other words, this second definition describes the actions of a person with an environmentalist worldview, which are embodied through "environmentalism."

Now because this second definition of environmentalism happens to fall closer in line with what most of us actually think when we hear the term "environmentalism" I feel that it doesn't need a whole lot of extra elaboration. I.e., it is rather self-explanatory. But just so I am being thorough enough, Brittanica formulated a much more detailed version of this second definition that might be a little easier to understand while also providing more context, and I think that it is important that you know that definition as well.

Environmentalism- *A political and ethical movement that seeks to improve and protect the quality of the natural environment through changes to environmentally harmful human activities; through the adoption of forms of political, economic, and social organization that are thought to be necessary for, or at least conducive to, the benign treatment of the environment by humans; and through a reassessment of humanity's relationship with nature. In various ways, environmentalism claims that living things other than humans, and the natural environment as a whole, are deserving of consideration in reasoning about the morality of political, economic, and social policies.* — Brittanica

There we go. Now we have two somewhat self-explanatory definitions of environmentalism. Thanks, Brittanica. Anyway, to keep things moving, you may have noticed, as I did, that there is a bit of a chicken and egg situation, it appears, going on between this second definition of environmentalism, and the definition of an environmentalist worldview, which is something notably different. What I mean by this is that environmentalism should, at least in theory, apply to both people who have an environmentalist worldview and those who do not, alike. This is to say that a completely bunk environment, or even just an environment that is difficult to thrive in, is not only something that runs contrary to what an environmentalist's goals are, but also something that hinders the heredity-centered efforts of those not concerned explicitly with the environment. In other words, there is quite a bit of overlap between the two because an environmentalist wants to protect the environment and make sure that it is ideal because that is, for lack of a better phrase, their ethos. However, environmentalists are not the only ones concerned with the environment because even people who are not explicitly concerned with environmentalism themselves still require an ideal, or at least livable environment if they are to succeed in whatever non-environmentalist endeavors they wish to succeed in. Like furthering bloodlines or building a legacy, for instance. So, when I say chicken and egg, I mean that both types of people, environmentalists, and non-environmentalists alike, still have the same inherent needs when it comes to preserving the environment. Ergo, the two definitions are similar, and in many ways connected, but with that said they are still notably different.

Now what this means to me is that it is logical to assume that we are all, to some degree or another, concerned with and reliant upon a clean and/or safe environment. Of course, this is kind of a pedantic point because, as I mentioned earlier in the side note, even though both sides of the aisle inherently want and need a clean environment they still seem to disagree about whether or not the environment is currently in danger, thus making one side far more likely to engage in environmentalist efforts than the other. I digress though.

Ok, now that we know what environmentalism actually is, and how it is different from an environmentalism worldview, in that one can care about the environment and environmentalism without being an environmentalist, I want to continue on and figure out if environmentalism as a whole is a new concept or instead something that has been around a while. To begin, as it turns out environmentalism is, surprisingly, not at all a new thing. In fact, it has been around in some form or another for thousands of years. For instance, 5,000 years ago in what is modern-day Pakistan the Indus civilization of Mohenjo Daro witnessed how manmade pollutants (primarily waste byproducts) were negatively affecting things in their community and this subsequently drove them to make novel strides in regard to irrigation, waste management, and sanitation. Furthermore, there was also a significant amount of environmentalism going on in ancient Greece back in the day. Now these efforts, instead of simply focusing on societal cleanliness, were primarily focused on land management, a much broader undertaking, and reviving the rural landscape, which at the time had been decimated by the hasty expansion of Grecian urban areas. Case in point, the famous philosopher Plato himself is quoted in his writings saying, "All the richer and softer parts have fallen away, and the mere skeleton of the land remains."

SIDENOTE

In addition to these two aforementioned cultures, the environmentalism cause has also been alive and well on our side of history. This is to say that since the beginning of the A.D. period (a little over 2000 years ago) the Romans, Chinese, Peruvians, Indians, and many other nations also began to have concerns about environmentalism as their societies grew, and according to historians, the reason for this is that these large and advanced civilizations, as they grew, began to notice new diseases forming, which were thriving/mutating in their unsanitary and densely populated urban areas. Furthermore, thanks to their exploding populations these civilizations also began to experience widespread soil erosion, which is where, essentially, the topsoil of an area gets overused and becomes devoid of the nutrients needed for farming. So yes, environmentalism is not new. Not broadly speaking anyway.

I could go on for days about this topic because there are many more examples of ancient cultures practicing environmentalism (see references if you are curious to know more) but suffice it to say that environmentalism has pretty much been a concern for societies for as long as humans have been building large man-made ecosystems that disrupt the natural status quo. The only difference now is the scale of our environment (i.e., the world is a much bigger place now than it was 2000 years ago), which has subsequently led to an increase in the scope of our preservation efforts, all of which currently strive to match that new, much larger landscape.

SIDENOTE

Even though many of the old examples of environmentalism more closely resemble conservationism, which is a specific subset of environmentalism that primarily seeks to manage natural resources in a specific area efficiently so that the people of that area do not expend all of their food and clean water, these examples show that those cultures still had a distinct concern for the preservation of their natural environments. Of course, as I just suggested, these early civilizations did not necessarily conceptualize the size and scope of the planet, or the broad negative impact certain human activities could have on it, but still, one would be hard-pressed to suggest that environmentalism is nothing more than a new-age hippy-dippy movement made by people who want to sit around and smoke grass in front of bulldozers. Rather, it is much more logical to suggest that most, if not all of the advanced civilizations of the past had at least some form of environmentalism, even if these efforts were only applied to their local areas.

Okay, moving on, now that we know what environmentalism is and that it has been around for quite some time, the next question I want to address is, "What does the current science say about environmentalism?" Good to go? Great. So, right off the bat let me say that, depending on what you mean by environmentalism (I.e., local or global environmentalism) there are actually several ways to look at this question. This is to say that, as I mentioned in the sidenote, much of the past environmentalism was actually more akin to local conservationism, not necessarily environmentalism, at least by today's standards that is, and if we are talking about environmentalism through this "think locally" conservationist style lens then this obviously is quite a bit different from, say, talking about global warming; mainly because this first type of environmentalism is something that we can all agree on and also something that we do not need a whole lot of science to understand. I.e., pretty much everyone knows the scientific reasons for indoor plumbing (sanitation) and wildlife tags (managing animal populations). Well, put plainly this local aspect of environmentalism is not really where the friction of the debate is and therefore looking at what science has to say about it would be, essentially, a waste of time. Rather, the main area where people seem to disagree is on the global environmentalism side. Hence, going forward we will be looking at this question from the perspective of someone focused on global environmentalism because this seems, at least to me, like a much more productive use of our time than, for instance, debating regulations on duck hunting in southern Kansas. Make sense?

Alright, so when it comes to global environmentalism, in essence the argument from the left side of the aisle (I am not going to say "broadly speaking" anymore when referring to the positions of the left and right, but just know that I still am.) is that humans are actively raising the Earth's temperature, thus causing man-made climate change (rising sea levels, mass extinction, etc.). Furthermore, the mechanism of this man-made climate change, according to that side, is something called the greenhouse effect. In other words, the crux of the left's position on global environmentalism is that humans are creating too many greenhouse gases and these gases are the root of the global climate problem. Now, what this means for us is that instead of asking "what does the science have to say about global environmentalism," the real question is "what is the greenhouse effect and what does the science say about that?"

Ok, so when it comes to the greenhouse effect, essentially, this is a three part process that results in heat energy from the sun getting trapped in our atmosphere, thus warming the planet to unnatural, and possibly detrimental levels. To explain, first, light energy from the sun passes through our atmosphere (only about 50% of it reaches the surface) and is then absorbed by the surface. Second, about 90% of that absorbed *light* energy is then radiated back out via infrared *heat* energy. Three, this infrared heat, which would normally pass easily through the atmosphere and back out into space, becomes trapped in the atmosphere because increased levels of greenhouse gasses (Carbon Dioxide, Methane, Nitrous Oxide, Chlorofluorocarbons, and excess water vapor), have filled that atmosphere to unnatural levels, thus causing that trapped energy to heat the entire planet like an oven. This, in lay terms, is the greenhouse effect. But is it really that big of a deal?

To answer that question as succinctly as possible, there is still a small segment of the scientific community that says the greenhouse effect is not happening, at least not to a noticeable degree, but for the most part the scientific consensus is that this process is, in fact, happening. More specifically, and this is coming from NASA itself, manmade activities such as burning fossil fuels, practicing deforestation, using aerosols, and increasing the overall surface area of agricultural land have increased the amount of greenhouse gases in the atmosphere by 50% since 1750. Furthermore, according to the data this has caused the planet's overall temperature to increase by 0.8-1.2 degrees Celsius, or 1.4-2.2 degrees Fahrenheit since the preindustrial age (mid-18th century). Now, at face value this may not seem like a lot, but according to many climate scientists if things continue as they are the planet is slated to increase by 1.5 degrees Celsius by the mid-21st century, and this is bad because, again, according to many climate scientists, if the planet's temperature increases by 2 degrees Celsius by the year 2100 then that level of increase within such a short period of time would cause massive problems like critical species extinctions, altered agricultural patterns, and rising seas levels that could, potentially, wipe out important coastal ecosystems and contaminate the freshwater sources used for irrigation and domestic farming. In other words, all of the mainstream data suggests that the greenhouse effect *is*, in fact, occurring, and this *will*, if it continues to occur, lead to serious issues within our food supplies and/or drinking water reservoirs. Pretty scary stuff, right?

At any rate, suffice it to say that all the evidence suggests that, yes, the greenhouse effect is real. Of course, even with all of that said I know that many people will still disagree that this is an actual problem, and frankly, given the inconsistencies with climate science in the past (the global cooling hoax) and the fact that scientists have also proven that the Earth experiences natural heating and cooling cycles that last thousands of years, I don't blame them. I mean, it is easy to discount this current greenhouse effect as "just another trend" when we can't really be sure how much climate change is natural and how much is man-made; but these contentions aside, I do want to say that a compelling bit of information that resonated with me in regard to this topic, and one that may sway you, was that the reason climate scientists blame humans for the increase in Earth's temperature, and not simply the natural solar cycle, is that we are only experiencing increased temperatures in the lower atmosphere and not the atmosphere as a whole. To go a little deeper, this is compelling, at least to me, because if the heat from the solar cycle (which we determine by measuring something called Total Solar Irradiance) was responsible for this increase in temperature then, in theory, we would see a somewhat even increase across all of the layers. Instead of this, though, we are currently seeing a cooling effect occurring in the upper layers of the atmosphere, while at the same time the lower ones are actually heating up. In lay terms, this just doesn't make sense if we are assuming that the natural solar cycle is the thing solely responsible for the increase in the Earth's temperature. Therefore, I do actually believe that at least some greenhouse effect is taking place. Still with me? Good just checking.

SIDENOTE

Just food for thought, the rate of atmospheric temperature increase has doubled since 1981 and the ten warmest years in the historical record have occurred since 2010. So, there is a direct correlation between the overall temperature of the planet and what we physically experience here on the ground.

Okay, so after that last paragraph I imagine some of you are pulling your hair out and yelling at me for being a bleeding heart tree hugger. Well, hold on just a second there, buddy! In all seriousness, I think that much of the current climate alarmism is overblown because, as we have seen since at least the 1970s, climate change has become very political in our modern world. This is to say that as far as environmentalism is concerned a lot of money and/or political power has been and currently still is involved. So, am I perturbed when I hear Representative Alexandria Ocasio Cortez proclaim that the Earth will end in ten years if we don't make immediate large-scale societal changes? No. But with that said, as a man of science who has also reviewed the published data for himself (see references if you would like to do the same), I do have to say that I am fairly certain that humans are causing at least some greenhouse effect with our emissions, and also that this is subsequently increasing the overall temperature of our planet, which could definitely, at a certain point, be detrimental to many aspects of our life here on this big ole blue rock. At any rate, when it comes to the science behind global environmentalism, put plainly, it is a "problem" that we should take into consideration. In other words, we cannot simply discount the pro-environmentalism side, and therefore it incumbent upon us to keep going. Capeesh? Sweet, then let's transition to the next topic we have to discuss. I.e., what role does the federal government have to play when it comes to environmentalism?

SIDENOTE

As I said earlier, all of us are, to one degree or another, concerned with the environment, both local and global; however, it is also true that the main point of contention between the two sides of the aisle is the severity of climate change. Along those same lines, look, there are a lot of really good arguments as to why global warming is not nearly as serious of a threat as the left makes it out to be. I recognize the validity of these, but the reason I did not spend time going over them is that, regardless of how severe manmade climate change actually is, I simply wanted to point out that it is a legitimate concept because, as a person trying to find a sane position on this issue, I wanted to first establish if the environmentalists even had a valid argument to begin with. Since they do, we can now easily move forward into how We the People should respond to the threat of manmade climate, regardless of how pressing that threat actually is. In other words, since we have established that this issue does, in fact, warrant discussion, we are now justified in discussing how the government should be involved because if it wasn't a legitimate concept, well, then the discussion could just end there. So, moving forward your own personal beliefs about the severity of global climate change are irrelevant, at least to me that is, because whether manmade climate change is an immediate threat to humanity or actually something that we don't really need to worry all that much about right now, it is still something that is likely happening, and therefore something that the government should consider. To that end, it is also something that they can and should regulate as well; but, of course, only in ways that We the People approve of. Anyway, this is all a long-winded way of saying that the government's involvement in the environmentalist effort is, in fact, a legitimate topic worthy of our attention. Good to go?

So, it is reasonable to assume that humans are likely contributing to global warming and that this can have a negative impact on our species, but what can and should the government do about it? Well, let me say first and foremost that I would rather fry up like a breakfast sausage before I approve of the Federal government stepping on anyone's constitutional rights and/or individual liberties, but with that said, I do still think that they have a legitimate role in protecting the environment, both locally (Clean water, sanitation, etc.) and globally (Greenhouse gas emissions, ocean ecosystems, etc.). To that end, though, as far as *what* the federal government's constitutional obligation is when it comes to the environment, well, technically there is none. This is to say that nowhere in the US Constitution does it explicitly say that a clean environment is a constitutional human right. Of course, with that said, though, this does not necessarily mean that the federal government is explicitly barred from protecting the environment either. I.e., Article IV Section 3 of the constitution, for instance, is a part of our founding documents that environmentalists have used to make the case that the government does, legally, have the power to protect the environment, and it is a part of our Constitution that I want to share with you now.

Article 4 Section 3: *New States may be admitted by the Congress into this Union; but no new State shall be formed or erected within the Jurisdiction of any other State; nor any State be formed by the Junction of two or more States, or Parts of States, without* *the Consent of the Legislatures of the States concerned as well as of the Congress.*

*The Congress **shall have Power to dispose of and make all needful Rules and Regulations respecting the Territory or other Property belonging to the United States**; and nothing in this Constitution shall be so construed as to Prejudice any Claims of the United States, or of any particular State.*

Alright, as you can see I highlighted the important part of this section, but for those who are listening, about two-thirds of the way down it is stated that Congress "shall have power to dispose of and make all needful rules and regulations respecting the territory and other property belonging to the United States." Now I am not a lawyer specializing in constitutional law, but it appears to me that this pretty clearly states that the federal government does, in fact, have the power to regulate how its land is managed, if for no other reason than to ensure that it is respected. But this wording is pretty vague, isn't it? I agree, it is. Therefore, a much more useable item found in our founding documents, at least in regard to the issue of environmentalism, is the Commerce Clause, which is found in Article 1 Section 8 of the US Constitution and also what I want to look at next.

Again, not a lawyer, but in essence this clause (which is shown below) gives the federal government the power to regulate any and all activities affecting commerce. Now the reason that this clause is important to environmentalists is that commerce, technically speaking, includes all pollution-causing items that cross state lines, and as you may have guessed, this includes automobiles and ships, as well as the items that those automobiles and ships are transporting.

For example, if a manufacturer creates pollution-causing products that contain forever chemicals (PFAS) and harmful aerosols, both of which have a well-documented negative impact on the environment, and then transports them across state lines, well, then those products fall under the purview of the commerce clause, thus legally making them the business of the federal government. Make sense?

SIDENOTE

For any of you nerds out there who want to make your own interpretations of this clause and how it applies to federal environmental regulations, this is the full commerce clause with additional details from Constitution.Congress.Gov.com. Now I used this source because it is actually rather handy for sane citizens concerned with environmental law in that if you see/hear a subsection that interests you, all you have to do is type the header of that section into Google and it will take you straight to the aforementioned website, which among other things, explains the cases and legislation surrounding each of the items (I.e., type in Artl.S8.C3.1 and you will find a full description of the overview of the commerce clause, as well as how many times it has been used by the Supreme Court.)

(Artl.S8.1 Overview of Congress's Enumerated Powers)

Article 1, Section 8, Clause 3:

"To regulate Commerce with foreign Nations, and among the several States, and with the Indian Tribes;"

Artl.S8.C3.1 Overview of Commerce Clause

Artl.S8.C3.2 Meaning of Commerce

Artl.S8.C3.3 Meaning of Among the Several States in the Commerce Clause

Continuing on, even though these are two very good constitutional tools for environmentalists to use in their fight for environmentalism, they are not necessarily foolproof in that there are also two potent legal weapons that have been used the other way to combat these federal powers. These are the Tenth Amendment and the supremacy clause (the second of which is located in Article VI Section 2 of the US Constitution). Just to lay it all out there, the Tenth Amendment states that "The powers not delegated to the United States by the Constitution, nor prohibited by it to the states, are reserved to the states respectively, or to the people." In other words, if an issue is not mentioned in the Constitution, it is then up to the individual states to decide on that issue. Now with that said, you still may be wondering how anti-environmentalists can use this amendment. I mean, after all, technically speaking there was no mention of environmentalism in this text either. Well, the reason it is useful for those wishing to ignore federal environmental regulations is that, as I said before, the environment is not clearly mentioned in the Constitution. So, this ambiguity leaves some legal wiggle room when it comes to certain environmental laws because defendants can and do make the case that states are the ones who actually have the ultimate say over their environmental laws, and not the federal government. Got it? Great, then let's move on to the second tool used to fight environmental laws.

The second weapon anti-environmentalists can and do use to fight federal environmental regulations is the supremacy clause. In essence, this clause states that "This Constitution, and the Laws of the United States which shall be made in Pursuance thereof; and all Treaties made, or which shall be made, under the Authority of the United States, shall be the supreme Law of the Land; and the Judges in every State shall be bound thereby, anything in the Constitution or Laws of any State to the Contrary notwithstanding." In other words, federal laws supersede state laws when there is a conflict. Now, if you are like me, at face value this also seems like a problem for states fighting federal environmental laws, right? Well, here is the caveat. You see, the supremacy clause only applies if the federal laws themselves are constitutional, which, again, brings us back to the somewhat questionable constitutionality of the federal government making and enforcing environmental laws in the first place. I.e., if the US Constitution doesn't mention environmentalism, are any environmental laws they pass actually constitutional? If not, well, then the supremacy clause would state that the individual states do, in fact, have the power to overrule these laws.

So, is the environment a state issue, or a federal one? Well, to be honest a compelling case can be made for both of these positions. This is to say that I *can* see the merit of a position wherein regulating environmental policy is the business of the individual states, and their alone, but I can also see the merit in a position wherein the federal government has the power to step in, when needed, for the welfare of the entire country's environment. With that said, though, I don't actually think we have to choose one or the other. In other words, perhaps these positions do not have to be mutually exclusive. You see, when it comes to who holds the reigns in regard to environmental policy, what I believe is that states can and should handle local environmentalism because there really is no need for the government to involve itself in such low-level issues. But at the same time I also believe that when it comes to environmental practices that affect things across state lines, such as managing interstate waterways or even global issues (like greenhouse gasses, for instance), the federal government has a legitimate role to play as well. Ergo, a sane citizen can logically hold both of these positions at once because, as we discussed earlier in the chapter, technically there are two types of environmentalism. I digress though.

Regardless of which particular argument you found to be the most compelling of these four, the truth is that they may all be, in a legal sense, irrelevant. I say this because after doing some more research into this topic I now think that, to a degree, all four of these arguments are actually superseded, in a way, by Section 1 of the 14th Amendment. Let me explain.

Section 1 of the 14th Amendment states that "All persons born or naturalized in the United States, and subject to the jurisdiction thereof, are citizens of the United States and of the State wherein they reside. **No State shall make or enforce any law which shall abridge the privileges or immunities of citizens of the United States; nor shall any State deprive any person of life, liberty, or property, without due process of law; nor deny to any person within its jurisdiction the equal protection of the laws."**

Once again, for those who are listening that is, I highlighted the portion of this section that states "No State shall make or enforce any law which shall abridge the privileges or immunities of citizens of the United States; nor shall any State deprive any person of life, liberty, or property, without due process of law; nor deny to any person within its jurisdiction the equal protection of the laws." because this is the important part when it comes to what the federal government can and cannot do in regard to regulating the environment. In lay terms, the federal government can, in fact, overstep a state's authority if that state is infringing upon its citizen's ability to engage in life, liberty, and the ownership of property. Now the Constitution is not the Muslim Quran, a text wherein if one passage contradicts another passage then the latter is said to take precedence, but the 14th Amendment was written after all of the other passages that we have reviewed. Therefore, I feel that it *is* logical to assume that this amendment is, at the very least, equally valid when compared to the others, if not more valid. Well, if this is the case, and legally speaking it seems to be that it is, then one could certainly make the argument that the federal government can and should ensure that all of its states provide an environment that does not inhibit the constitutional rights of its citizens. In other words, based on the 14th Amendment the federal government would have a legitimate case if it were to step in and prevent a state from, let's say, contaminating its drinking water because this would impede the ability of that state's citizens to live freely.

SIDENOTE

Life, liberty, and the right to own property is a little different than "life, liberty, and the pursuit of happiness," but the latter phrase is used in the Declaration of Independence. So don't get too hung up on that because both wordings are still located within our founding documents and both, though they are not exactly the same, share a similar sentiment.

Alright, we have covered a lot, though due to time constraints not in as much detail as I wish we could have, but I think it is fair to say that thus far we have established,

1) *The environment, local and global, is, to some degree or another, all of our concern; and this applies to both those who have an environmentalist worldview and those who do not, alike.*

2) *The science, though somewhat inconsistent over the last 50 years, does make a reasonable case that there probably is at least some degree of negative manmade climate change occurring.*

3) *The federal government, though not given explicit constitutional power in regard to climate regulations, does have a legitimate role in ensuring a clean and safe environment for its citizens, and, thanks to the 14th Amendment, at least some constitutional power to do so.*

With all of this said, though, we have yet to establish what a sane position is when it comes to the issue of environmentalism. Well, along those same lines when it comes to establishing this sane position we could get into all of the current and pending legislation that has to do with environmentalism, as well as what we think about the Environmental Protection Agency (EPA), but I think that, like we did with the other issues we have covered thus far, a better idea is to leave that region/issue-specific research up to you and instead establish a sane position regarding environmental regulation as a whole. Especially since I am by no means a legal expert on every one of these specific pieces of legislation. So, without further to do, let's get into it and wrap this thing up.

SIDENOTE

Even though we are not going to go into all of the specific legislation involving climate change, here are some of the big ones for those of you who are curious.

Source: https://constitution.laws.com/the-supreme-court/environment

The Clean Air Act (CAA) 1970 – A Federal law that regulates air emissions. It also authorizes the EPA (Environmental Protection Agency) to establish quality standards that protect society and regulate hazardous air pollutants.

The Clean Water Act (CWA) 1972 – Developed a basic structure to discharge pollutants and regulate quality in surface waters.

The United States Environmental Protection Agency (EPA) – Protects human health and the natural environment. Congress gave the EPA authority to write regulations explaining what is needed to improve and implement environmental laws.

Energy Policy Act (EPA) – Addresses the issues concerning the production of energy in the US including all aspects of energy efficiency, renewable energy, oil and gas, coal, vehicles and motor fuels, hydropower, geothermal energy, and climate change technology.

Food Quality Protection Act (1996) – This Act was created to evaluate the levels of pesticide residues in foods to meet the standard of public health protection.

Safe Drinking Water Act (1974) – This Act establishes the standards for safe drinking tap water requiring rules for groundwater protection. Last amended in 1996 with funds established to pay for water system upgrades.

So, it appears to me that the main issue with the federal government's attempts to regulate the environment is that, as with all things the federal government is involved in, there is a large degree of corruption, inefficiency, and overall impracticality inherent to their approaches. Take, as two examples, the current administration's plan to make half of all vehicles on the road electric by 2030 and the Environmental Protection Agencies' (EPA) hatred of nuclear power plants. Now at face value these seem like good ideas, right? Well, the truth is that, regardless of how they may look on the surface, neither of these ideas actually are good. For one, when it comes to electric cars their batteries require rare earth metals, which require a lot of water to mine, and therefore their production contributes to a ton of soil contamination and/or water table pollution. Furthermore, the manufacturing process for these batteries also creates a lot of negative byproducts, not the least of which is carbon. How much carbon you ask? Well, there is some conflicting information on this so I won't give hard numbers, but overall the consensus seems to be that manufacturing an electric car battery in a factory, which is over 1000 lbs. when it is finished, will release somewhere around as much carbon as a fossil fuel vehicle burns over the course of 8 years. So, in other words, a lot. At any rate, if you add all of that up and then factor in that the disposal of these batteries is a complete nightmare due to all of their toxicity, you quickly see that electric cars, technically, aren't really all that green. In other words, they may seem like they make a huge impact on greenhouse gas emissions and the overall levels of pollution, but the reality is that they don't.

Moving on to nuclear, when it comes to the Environmental Protection Agencies' outright disdain for this type of energy, their anti-nuclear position doesn't make much sense either, from an environmentalist standpoint that is. You see, we have all been taught to be deathly afraid of nuclear energy because, I mean, who wants another Chernobyl, right? Well, put plainly the reality is that well-regulated nuclear plants are one of if not the cleanest and safest forms of energy that we have; and, just as a bonus, they are also far more efficient than your average green energy source. So much more so, in fact, that it actually takes 300 square miles of renewable energy sources (windmills and solar panels) to make the same amount of energy that only 1 square mile of nuclear plant makes, and the nuclear plant, I might add, does all of this without needing any of the rare earth metals that windmills and solar panels rely on. But more than all of that, 90% of all of our goods here in the US are transported by ship during at least some point in their life, and these vessels account for around 3% of our overall C02 emissions. Well, I don't know about you, but from my point of view it seems like an easy solution for these emissions would be to simply convert these ships into vessels that, instead of diesel, run on clean and efficient nuclear energy, which is something many ships already run on, and quite successfully I might add. Anyway, all of this is to say that, put frankly, many of the government's current environmental efforts do not actually remedy the problems that environmentalism seeks to solve. Rather, it seems like they are more often than not an exercise in futility that is plagued and/or driven by political theatre and governmental corruption/incompetence.

SIDENOTE

The biggest causes of carbon emissions around the world are:

Electricity & Heat (25%)

Agriculture, Forestry & other land use (24%)

Industry (21%)

Transportation (14%)

Other energy (10%

Buildings (6%)

According to my analyses, most of these sectors, if not all, would be far cleaner and more efficient if the goal was to incorporate nuclear energy into them instead of electric/renewable energy sources because this would decrease fossil fuel emissions, and subsequently greenhouse gas emissions, while also giving us reliable and predictable energy; and this also applies to the second item on the list (Agriculture, Forestry & other land use) in that nuclear would have a much smaller impact (1/300th) on the land environment than renewable energy sources (solar panels and windmills) would, thus decreasing carbon emissions from that source to nearly zero.

Alright, so with everything we have covered thus far, we are left in a little bit of a conundrum here, at least when it comes to finding a sane position that is. This is to say that on one hand, the federal government, as well as us, should care about protecting the environment. However, on the other hand, we see that the environmental legislation getting proposed and/or passed by the federal government, or at least most of it, is, to put it lightly, bullshit. So what is a sane position on environmentalism?

In lay terms, the sane position is that we absolutely do need to ensure that corporations and/or manufacturers are not destroying our environment, be it our local environment or the global environment (Well, our part of it anyway. There is a strong case to be made that we should do something about China, which is absolutely blowing us out of the water in terms of greenhouse gas emissions and overall water contamination), and believing this doesn't make you a tree hugger, or a bleeding heart liberal, it simply makes you practical. Now, when it comes to what specific regulations are required to do this, well, again, in lay terms, that should be up to We the People. I.e., We the people have a responsibility to look at the data, determine what environmental policies are economically feasible, and then sensibly regulate the environment without going insane like the current climate alarmists.

Of course, with that said there is an important caveat that comes with this position. This is to say that if we are to actually do this then we must first and foremost regain control over the currently unchecked bureaucrats making our environmental policy. In other words, if We the People are going to take even one step in the direction of responsibly preserving our environment then we must first demand the immediate removal of all unelected bureaucrats running the EPA, because these people should be beholden to us, and not whoever is currently in charge of the federal government. Now with that said, I am not naïve and I know that this last part is easier said than done, but be that as it may, let me just remind you that, as I have said many times in this book, We the People can and do influence our elected leaders, even if it doesn't always seem like it. Ergo, if our goal is to abolish the current EPA and replace it with an organization run by officials, we ourselves elected, then let your leaders know because if you make it an issue, I promise that they will too. Anyhow, that is the end of the chapter. I hope you got something out of it, even though I did not have nearly enough space to get as technical as I wanted, but if not stay tuned because we still have quite a bit more to discuss in this book and I am sure you will find at least some of it interesting.

In closing, let me leave you with just a few things to remember. First, as sane citizens we should all care about the environment, even if this forces us to temporarily feel like the obnoxious climate alarmists that we all know and hate (Looking at you Greta Thunberg and Leonardo Decaprio.). This is because there is at least some credence to the idea that we either currently are, or potentially could harm our planet to such a degree that it hinders the American citizenry's ability to engage in life, liberty, and the pursuit of happiness. Second, the federal government does, technically, have the constitutional power to legislate environmental policy, but let us not forget that even with this power they are still constitutionally beholden to the wills and desires of We the People. So, with all of that said, let us, the sane citizens, stop this issue from becoming a partisan weapon that can be used by corrupt actors pursuing sinister means. Instead, let's all take the sane position of restructuring the EPA and making sure that We the People, based on our own mental cognizance and ability to interpret the scientific data for ourselves, get to decide who runs the EPA, which environmental policies they get to pass, and last but not least, which ones they cannot.

CHAPTER 7

Immigration

"New York City is, and has always been, a city of immigrants. We are a destination for diversity and a place where people from every nation seek refuge, raise families, and enrich our communities. Under my administration, our government will reflect that."

—NYC Mayor Eric Adams (June 2021)

"We need to ensure that [undocumented immigrants] receive healthcare and protection…that ICE is never in a position to partner with the police department and harm them."

—NYC Mayor Eric Adams (June 2021)

"[That is] our responsibility as a city, I'm proud that this is a right-to-shelter state and we're going to continue to do that. New York is a city that has always represented the democratic values and the values of our city of showing compassion, and that's what we're doing today."

—NYC Mayor Eric Adams (August 2021)

"We should protect our immigrants. Period. Yes, New York City will remain a sanctuary city under an Adams administration."

—NYC Mayor Eric Adams (October 2021)

"I'm speaking directly to the administration. This is a problem that we must have a resolution both from Congress on immigration, but [also] the administration to deal with the immediate need that we have."

—NYC Mayor Eric Adams (January 2023)

"This cannot continue. It's not sustainable, and we're not going to pretend as though it is sustainable. This is wrong that New York City is carrying the weight of a national problem."

—NYC Mayor Eric Adams (July 2023)

"Never in my life have I had a problem that I didn't see an ending to. I don't see an ending to this. This issue will destroy New York City. We're getting 10,000 migrants a month. … people all over the globe have made their minds up that they're going to come through the southern part of the border and come into New York City."

—NYC Mayor Eric Adams (September 2023)

"Every community in this city is going to be impacted. We have a $12 billion deficit that we're going to have to cut – every service in this city is going to be impacted."

—NYC Mayor Eric Adams (September 2023)

"The city we knew, we're about to lose."

—NYC Mayor Eric Adams (September 2023)

If you read all of those aforementioned quotes in their entirety then you undoubtedly noticed, as I did, a drastic shift between how 2021 Mayor Adam's viewed immigration and how 2023 Mayor Adam's viewed it. This change is odd, isn't it? I mean, to go from being such an outspoken supporter of illegal immigration to saying it will destroy your city in only two years, what the hell happened? Well, if I'm being honest it actually isn't all that complicated. Put plainly, in 2022 some of the border states (primarily Texas and Florida) got fed up with states (primarily New York and California) that were nowhere near the border talking non-stop about how cruel having a strong border was and thus began bussing all of their illegal immigrants north; and, as you can see from the quotes listed above, this led to some Democrat leaders learning the hard way that being light on illegal immigration doesn't work so well when you actually have to deal with the issue yourself.

Now the reason I wanted to show these specific examples of Mayor Adams shifting his position on this issue wasn't to make an inadvertent campaign ad for his upcoming political opponent. Rather, I did it because I wanted to demonstrate how open borders, though a good idea in theory, do not actually work in real life, and everybody, left, right, and center knows it. At any rate, let's move on.

The next issue we are going to discuss in this book is one that has divided Republicans and Democrats for many years, but especially so since the Trump administration, an administration that, among other things, got elected on the back of slogans like "Build the wall" and "We will build a big, beautiful wall and Mexico will pay for it." Now, this would not have been a particularly inflammatory platform for a candidate to run on just a few years earlier; however, as you may well remember, if you were into US politics at that time, is that this specific platform received stark criticism from the left side of the political aisle and even resulted in half of the country's elected leaders calling then-Candidate Trump a xenophobe, and a racist. More than that, though, these criticisms against Trump were so aggressive, inflammatory, and more importantly effective that following this election they managed to permeate far beyond the presidential election and even years later (and to this day I might add) they were making their way down to the local level and being used as a political weapon against anyone right of center. For instance, during the 2018 mid-term elections even my front door, which was all the way down in Austin Texas at the time, was constantly covered in pamphlets that showed children in cages accompanied by the phrase "Vote Democrat in 2018…. You know why." Pretty intense, yeah? Anyway, the issue that I am referring to is immigration and it is, to put it lightly, a doozy.

Now at the outset, before we begin analyzing this issue I want to first say that going over the non-US history of immigration is, for this chapter, unnecessary. Yes, I know that generally I prefer to cover the non-US history of issues at least briefly before finding a sane position on them, but the reason that this one is different is that, put frankly, throughout all of human history not a single advanced civilization has forgone having a border. This is to say that no one, not even the most liberal of nations, has ever decided that having open borders is a *good* and/or sustainable policy, and this is not only true for nations that have robust social safety net policies, like the United States, for instance, but also for ancient civilizations in which there were no such protections. Ergo, suffice it to say that it is not xenophobic, nor racist to believe in a strong border, it is just the way the world works, and therefore there is no reason to spend our valuable time digging through historical examples in order to justify why it is a good idea for nations to have one. Good to go? Great, then let's keep going.

SIDENOTE

Right off the bat I wanted to explicitly detail what constitutional power the government actually has in regard to regulating immigration. Now because my areas of expertise are in political science, psychology, and political psychology, not the law, I figured that instead of giving you my version of an analysis, I would give you a description of these powers that come from a legal source instead.

Source: Constitution.congress.gov.com

Article I, Section 8, Clause 18:

[The Congress shall have Power . . .] To make all Laws which shall be necessary and proper for carrying into Execution the foregoing Powers, and all other Powers vested by this Constitution in the Government of the United States, or in any Department or Officer thereof.

Long-standing Supreme Court precedent recognizes Congress as having plenary power over immigration, giving it almost complete authority to decide whether foreign nationals (aliens, under governing statutes and case law) may enter or remain in the United States. But while Congress's power over immigration is well established, defining its constitutional underpinnings is more difficult. The Constitution does not mention immigration, but parts of the Constitution address related subjects. The Supreme Court has sometimes relied upon Congress's powers over naturalization (the term and conditions in which an alien becomes a U.S. citizen), foreign commerce, and, to a lesser extent, upon the Executive Branch's implied Article II foreign affairs power, as sources of federal immigration power. While these powers continue to be cited as supporting the immigration power, since the late nineteenth century, the Supreme Court has described the power as flowing from the Constitution's establishment of a federal government. The United States government possesses all the powers incident to a sovereign, including unqualified authority over the Nation's borders and the ability to determine whether foreign nationals may come within its territory. The Supreme Court has generally assigned the constitutional power to regulate immigration to Congress, with executive authority mainly derived from congressional delegations of authority.

In exercising its power over immigration, Congress can make laws concerning aliens that would be unconstitutional if applied to citizens. The Supreme Court has interpreted that power to apply with most force to the admission and exclusion of nonresident aliens abroad seeking to enter the United States. The Court has further upheld laws excluding aliens from entry on the basis of ethnicity, gender and legitimacy, and political belief. It has also upheld an Executive Branch exclusion policy, premised on a broad statutory delegation of authority, that some evidence suggested was motivated by religious animus. But the immigration power has proven less than absolute when directed at aliens already physically present within the United States. Even so, the Supreme Court's jurisprudence reflects that Congress retains broad power to regulate immigration and that the Court will accord substantial deference to the government's immigration policies, particularly those that implicate matters of national security.

##

In other words, the government, constitutionally speaking, can and should regulate immigration based upon what is good for We the People. Furthermore, the government, so long as it does not infringe upon any one's *human* rights does not have to afford non-citizen immigrants the same constitutional rights that We the People are granted.

Ok, so even though I just said that we don't *need* to justify why having a strong border is, overall a good and sane idea, it is important to note right from the get-go, for our purposes that is, that legal immigration and illegal immigration are not by any means the same thing. What I mean by this is that, for all of the negative aspects of illegal immigration, which are somewhat self-evident (terrorists entering the country unchecked, an increased burden on social welfare programs, an incentive for criminal organizations to engage in human trafficking, etc.), there are just as many if not more positive aspects of legal immigration. To list just a few, legal immigration increases the working population of the US, which subsequently increases our economic capacity as well as our senior-to-working-age ratio, it incentivizes the best and brightest from all over the world to come to and/or invest in our nation, which subsequently makes the US more competitive on the international stage when it comes to technology and STEM fields, and furthermore, even legal immigrants who are less likely to be involved in these high-skilled fields typically still, more often than not, have high levels of ambitious and/or an entrepreneurial spirit, which subsequently leads to them going on to create businesses and/or products, all of which will end up contributing to the overall growth of our nations GDP. Ergo, as you can see immigration, if done properly, can have quite a positive effect on our country. But be that as it may, what is the proper way to do it? In other words, if immigration in and of itself is neither wholly good nor wholly bad, what is the best overall way to handle it as a nation? Well, discounting those who do not want immigration based solely on the fact that they dislike people of other ethnicities, it seems to me that the main disagreement between the two sides of the political aisle in regard to this question is not whether or not we should allow immigration, but rather *who* should be allowed to immigrate to the US, and how many of those people we can take.

Now before moving on I would like to point out that, in order to find a solution to these two points of contention we first need to know who the *who* is when we are talking about immigration. And I will also point out that, by default, this means that supporting a weak border, and by proxy illegal immigration, in any capacity is not only impractical but also insane because this actually destroys the validity and effectiveness of *all* legal immigration policies outright. In other words, without a strong border any prospective immigrants out there looking to come to the US, due to the inherent realities of human nature will rather obviously be incentivized to take the path of least resistance (i.e., immigrating illegally) over the more difficult legal route (legal immigration), thus giving us here on our side of the border little to no insight and/or control over who the *who* is in the immigration debate, which, again, is the literal point of an immigration policy in the first place. Ergo, regardless of whether the immigration process does or does not need to be reformed (it does), this does not change the fact that we also need a strong border, as well as one that is enforced. Simple enough?

Alright, now that we have a rough understanding of the difference between legal and illegal immigration, as well as why we need a strong border, let's keep things rolling along by talking about some of the notable changes/legal battles that took place throughout our nation's history in regard to this issue so that we can better determine whether the current immigration policies we have need an adjustment, or if they are fine where they are.

SIDENOTE

Just FYI.

"Three fundamental concepts underlie U.S. citizenship law, and their relative importance shifts depending on the needs and the norms of the era. The first is *jus soli*, the right of the soil, which means that those born on U.S. soil are automatically granted citizenship. The second is *jus sanguinis*, the right of blood, which means that those born to U.S. citizens in other countries automatically earn U.S. citizenship under most conditions. **The third is pledged allegiance, whereby those who civically commit to the United States become U.S. citizens. Pledged allegiance is related to the concept of naturalization, the process by which an immigrant voluntarily moves to the United States and swears allegiance to the government to fully enter American political life through citizenship."**
—Cato Institute

P.S. That third concept is the one most pertinent to this chapter and therefore is the one you need to take note of.

To begin, as fate would have it immigration has been a fairly major political concern in the United States since pretty much the very beginning. For example, in 1790, only three years after the US Constitution was officially ratified, Congress passed something called the Naturalization Act of 1790. Now the primary purpose of this act, which was motivated by people like Thomas Jefferson who, prior to its passage stated that "the present desire of America is to produce rapid population, by as great importations of foreigners as possible" was, essentially, to extend "citizenship to free white persons of good character who had resided in the United States for two years and took an oath of allegiance." In other words, this act was passed because many of the original leaders of the country felt that creating a boom in the US population would, in theory, help the country pay off its leftover debt from the American Revolution and increase its overall labor force; and to put it lightly, even though it did have quite a few personnel restrictions ("white persons" only), it actually ended up working rather well. So well, in fact, that some of those early leaders actually started feeling like its success was rapidly creating a national security threat.

Essentially, the logic behind this new fear was that having such a large, foreign-born population with voting rights could potentially open up the country to detrimental levels of foreign influence; and as a result of these concerns five years later the aforementioned Naturalization Act of 1790 was subsequently removed and in its place Congress passed the updated Naturalization Act of 1795. Now unlike the previous act of 1790, which primarily sought to *bolster* immigration, this new one actually tried to *reduce* the flow of new immigrants, and it did this by expanding the restrictions of that previous act. This is to say that, among other things, this new "updated" act increased "the residency requirement for naturalization to five years and added a clause requiring prospective citizens to declare their intention to naturalize three years before doing so." Furthermore, it also made things a bit more restrictive by adding in a new "religious and moral subtext that changed 'good character' to 'good moral character'," which is really just another way of saying that not only do you have to be white to immigrate here, but you also have to be a Christian. Ergo, even though immigration didn't stop post-1795, it did significantly slow.

Ok, moving on, from this period in America's infancy until about 1815 the immigration debate was, as far as the debate stage went, quite lively, but with that said, legislatively speaking very little actually changed. Sure, there were various increases and decreases in the amount of time it took to become a naturalized citizen, and the federal government also attempted to impose various "safety" restrictions that served the purpose of preventing indentured servants and poor immigrants from being able to come to the country, but overall immigration was welcomed in the US and, to a certain class of people, fairly easy. Well, despite this period of steady, albeit slow increases in the immigrant population, around 1830 immigration saw an unprecedented spike. This is to say that between 1830 and the 1840's the number of immigrants in the US soared from a measly 599,125 to an immense 1,713,251 driven primarily by the Irish potato famine of 1845 and/or various European revolutions that were taking place at the time (1948); and this this drastic increase in immigrants was so intense that it actually ended up causing certain members of Congress to, once again, attempt to raise the period of time it took to become a naturalized citizen (twenty-one years this time).

Well, even with this unprecedented boom in immigration, just like the past attempts to "stem the flow" had failed, these new attempts failed as well, in part due to that fact that at this time things in the government moved much slower than they do today, and also because this second, much more rapid wave of immigration had already begun to naturally slow by the 1850s, thus making it a proverbial flash in the pan as far as political issues went at the time. With that said, though, I still wanted to mention this occurrence in our immigration history because, even though this was not a particularly consequential time for immigration, from a policy perspective that is, it did mark a notable shift in the way that the culture viewed the issue. In other words, by the end of this period even many of the "average Joe's" were beginning to have deep-seated concerns over largescale immigration, which was not previously the case, and this likely planted the seeds for the anti-immigration sentiments that were to come later on.

Anyway, continuing on, these newly founded concerns over the 1830 immigration spike ended up being temporarily overshadowed in 1861 when the Civil War broke out and many of our nation's leaders, including Abraham Lincoln, began to reverse their views on the controversial issue. This is to say that after the Civil War broke out there was a massive surge in the need for industrial labor, which subsequently caused the government to start welcoming immigrants with open arms, and the people followed suit. Of course, be this as it may (Don't call me woke! It's just an interesting aspect of the history of this time period), I do have to point out that even with this need for a bolstered labor force, given the time period legislators still maintained their preference for "whites" of "good moral standing." Ergo, it wasn't necessarily a deep-seated structural change in the nation's views on immigration, which as we will see did end up happening later on, but rather a surface-level one that was inspired primarily by the war effort. I digress though.

Unfortunately, for the immigrants of the time that is, this requirement/enthusiasm for new laborers evaporated rather quickly after the war ended (1865), and therefore, just as quickly as immigration had been a good thing in the eyes of the nation, it once again became a bad thing, only this time, as I said before, the population was concerned about immigration as well. Anyway, this revitalized anti-immigration sentiment actually ended up being the new status quo in the country for quite some time. In fact, until the end of

WWII the goal of US immigration policy was primarily centered around decreasing the abilities of foreign-born individuals to gain citizenship, not increasing them, and these efforts only got starker as time went on. Now I won't get into all of these goings-on here because that could be a chapter in and of itself, so for parsimony, suffice it to say that from the mid-19th century even up until and after the First World War a plurality of America's leaders (and the "average Joe's") were, put plainly, staunchly anti-immigration; though, ironically, they also began to grant black Americans citizenship during this time period (Naturalization Act of 1870) which made them what, anti-immigration progressives? Hmmm, what a weird time period. Any who, the overall takeaway from this section is that for most of America's pre-WWII history immigration was seen, primarily, as a net negative by its inhabitants. Good to go? Great, then let's move on to when things really started to change in the US, at least on the immigration front that is.

To begin, by the time WWII had officially ended the nation's long-standing anti-immigration sentiment unexpectedly started to undergo a significant change/reversal, and the reason for this sudden change, in lay terms, was that following that war the Holocaust, which very few Americans had known about before and during the war, started to get a lot of national attention. Now this occurrence was significant to the immigration debate because, considering America's, at that time, somewhat longstanding trend of being anti-immigration (even throughout the First World War in which millions of Europeans had become defunct refugees), when this realization of the horrors of the Holocaust became common knowledge, to put it lightly the US was left with quite a bit of egg on its face. Said another way, after WWII America was made by the international community to feel a great deal of shame over its harsh prewar immigration policies because these policies had undoubtedly been responsible for leaving many German and Polish Jews unable to leave Europe for the safety of the US, even as they were being killed in droves. Ergo, this "national shame" impacted the American population deeply and this subsequently led to a deep-seated change in the country's overall view on immigration.

SIDENOTE

As a result of this post-WWII shame two official acts were quickly passed by US legislators, the Displaced Persons Act of 1948, and the Refugee Relief Act of 1953, and these acts, among other things, allowed over half a million refugees into the country, attempted to combat the Soviet's Communist propaganda, and also removed the preexisting citizenship bans on Asian-born individuals. Now I do have to point out that these acts were not the first pro-immigration reforms our country saw (remember the original purpose of the Naturalization Act of 1790), and they also were not the last, but with that said they do still mark a pivotal time in our nation's immigration debate. This is because these pieces of legislation were not passed simply because of economic and/or ethnic/social reasons, which most of the reforms of the past were, but rather because the culture of the nation was beginning to adopt a more liberal position on the issue of immigration. Anyway, my point is that even though they do not seem that important and/or noteworthy on the surface, if you look under that surface the passage of these acts was actually indicative of a rather consequential cultural shift, at least when it came to the issue of immigration that is.

Alright, continuing ever onward, in the years following this notable post-WWII culture change, policy began, as it generally does, to follow the will of the people, and this culture/policy trend continued through most of the 20th and 21st centuries. In other words, after WWII things in the immigration realm began to move evermore to the "liberal" side of things. Now, once again, due to space restrictions we can't get into everything that happened on the immigration front during that roughly 80-year period, but with that said I still want to cover at least a few of the wavetops because some of the things that happened during this period are still quite relevant today. Sound like a plan? Alright, let's get into it then, shall we?

Starting near the beginning of that aforementioned period, during and after the Second World War our southern border saw quite a bit of action on the immigration front, and this action, combined with the post-war cultural changes I just mentioned, eventually led to the passage of something called the Bracero Act (1942). In essence, this act functioned as a work visa program and it worked splendidly at stopping illegal immigration while also allowing the nation to reap all of the benefits of having a robust and regulated immigrant workforce. In other words, the Bracero Act allowed migrant workers from Mexico to legally work within the United States, primarily during specific harvest seasons, despite them not possessing full-on citizenship. Pretty smart, yeah?

Well, unfortunately, despite the relative success of the Bracero Act, and all of the positive benefits it had on the country (As we saw in 1865 a bolstered immigrant labor force can be quite handy, especially in times of war.), the program was started and stopped several times over the following 30 years and eventually, in 1964, it was shut down completely. Now the problem with this inconsistency in the Bracero Act's application is that at all of these points in which it was stopped, and certainly after it was disbanded altogether, illegal immigration saw notable spikes because at these points of inaction the act was not replaced with an alternative. Ergo, the already existing economic/cultural infrastructure of farmers looking for seasonal labor, something the Bracero Act had actually helped create and expand, simply decided to go underground since, at the end of the day, this process was still more efficient than following any of the new laws, which, in the views of the people affected (farmers and laborers) were just going to change again in a few years anyway. Put another way, the decision(s) to pause/stop the Bracero Act, and act that was effectively curbing illegal immigration when it was active, actually ended up making the problem way worse. Good job, government....

Alright, another notable point in the post-WWII immigration era was 1952, wherein the Immigration and Nationality Act of 1952 was passed. In essence, this act was an attempt by the law makers at that time to try and increase legal immigration, while also decreasing illegal immigration, which had begun to see regular spikes thanks to the aforementioned inconsistency of the Bracero Act. Well, unfortunately, despite moving in the right direction, from a sane citizen's perspective that is, this act was still severely flawed in that the strategy it used to regulate immigration was to enforce something called regional quotas. I.e., each country/region had a different number of immigrants that they were allowed to send as opposed to evaluating each immigrant on an individual basis, regardless of where they are from. Now I know that this strategy may look good on the surface, but be that as it may the problem with this regional quota system, from a purely strategic perspective that is, was that this type of method for handling immigration actually ended up incentivizing illegal immigration because, when it came to the US at the time, the lion's share of the regional quotas went to European nations; and this was a problem because, whether this strategy was simply designed to preserve the culture of the US, or a more sinister plan to preserve the predominantly white ethnicity of the nation, what it actually resulted in was individuals from the countries with low quotas (I.e., Eastern Hemisphere and Latin American countries) giving up on legal immigration altogether and instead pursuing alternative (illegal) means of entering the country. Ergo, the whole thing, like the Bracero Act, eventually backfired and actually made the problem it was trying to solve worse.

SIDENOTE

Now, with a strong border in place this quota system may have actually worked because illegal immigration would have been, essentially, a non-factor. But with that said, as I discuss in the next paragraph this was not the case at the time. I.e., the border was very weak at this time, and as a result when people *were* incentivized to emigrate illegally, they did so, and quite easily I might add.

Continuing on, eventually this quota-centric strategy was abandoned for a more progressive system with the passing of the Immigration and Nationality Act of 1965. Overall, this new act, among a few other things, tried to correct the "xenophobia" of the 1952 act, which had become a major talking point at this time thanks to the civil rights movement, by reversing the previous preference for Western immigrants, establishing a favorable preference for immigrants from the Eastern Hemisphere, and also by doing away with the regional quotas, thus allowing immigrants to "stand on their own merits". Hmmm, seems pretty fair, right? I mean, if you shunned other countries' immigrants in the past, why not make up for it by giving them better treatment now? Well, as fate would have it this plan by the legislature did not pan out exactly how they had hoped (I am starting to see a trend here….). You see, even though this act *did* allow non-Westerners into the country, it also implemented the same strict personal standards on those wishing to immigrate that the 1952 act had. In other words, if you were wealthy, highly educated, and/or possessed a rare skill, you were very likely to get in. However, if you not one of these "elites," eh, not so much. I.e., the problem with the Immigration and Nationality Act of 1965, at least when it comes to quelling illegal immigration that is, is that it did very little for unskilled and/or uneducated migrants. Of course, one could argue that this makes sense. Basically, that we only want the best and brightest from other countries, but with that said, given the meager strength of our southern border at the time (less than 4,000 agents compared to the over 19,000 protecting that same area today), this act actually had a negative impact on the country because in the end what it actually did was incentivize unskilled and uneducated immigrants to try and illegally cross our southern border, while also not doing anything to tactically prepare for that inevitable surge. Ergo, illegal immigration continued to rise during this period because, just like the Immigration and Nationality Act of 1952 was an abstract failure, so too was the Immigration and Nationality Act of 1965.

SIDENOTE

Follow-on acts, such as the Immigration Act of 1990 tried to further liberalize the immigration policy in much the same way that the 1965 act did, however, the same problems still remained. The reason for this was that, essentially, the border was not very secure during this period and there also wasn't a very strong framework for unskilled and uneducated migrants to use. In other words, we had/have a system wherein the border was/is not only weak, but also the only *practical* option for unskilled and uneducated individuals seeking to immigrate here. Sound like a recipe for success to you? I didn't think so. Anyway, that wraps up most of the notable points in the immigration debate post-WWII. Now let's change direction and look at the immigration debate in more recent history.

Ok, moving on, after the Immigration and Nationality Act of 1965 several more acts were passed and with their passage the immigration debate continued moving in a progressive direction, albeit slowly, all the way through the 1990s. With this said, though, following 9/11 this changed and the entire immigration landscape experienced some very potent reforms. To explain, after our beloved towers fell in 2001 policymakers and politicians alike began to face two incompatible national desires. This is to say that, on the one hand, the population was moving ever onward toward more progressive stances on immigration, but on the other hand, immigration was beginning to be looked upon with a somewhat fearful gaze because in the wake of 9/11 everyone was hyper-concerned with the threat of terrorism. Well, unsurprisingly this state of dissonant ideologies among the electorate rather quickly resulted in the rhetoric/actions of the politicians of that time (Bush, Obama, etc.) becoming somewhat two-faced when it came to immigration. In other words, after 9/11 both the Bush and Obama administrations had to somehow balance the electorates' desire to open our borders to *good* migrants while also making sure that we all felt secure. Ergo, after those aforementioned attacks we ended up with some strange and counterintuitive situations like Obama deporting so many illegal immigrants that he garnered the nickname "Deporter in Chief," while at the same time he was also putting into place things like the Deferred Action for Childhood Arrivals (DACA) policy, a policy that, among other things, made it easier for young illegals born in the US to become citizens; which also incidentally opened many legal loopholes for their parents to achieve citizenship and/or permanent resident status as well. Anyway, the moral of the story is that after 9/11 the post-WWII pro-immigration trend began to compete with concerns of national security (as had happened after the Naturalization Act of 1790 if you remember), and the result was a tumultuous bi-partisan battle between two competing political narratives (I.e., pro-immigration and anti-immigration).

Now an interesting aspect of this time period, at least to me, is that at this point in our recent history most people on the left and right sides of the aisle actually had similar views on immigration. This is to say that both sides believed that illegal immigration was a problem while also believing that serious reform was needed to help those seeking to enter the country legally. Of course, be that as it may, unfortunately we never actually got to see where this dichotomous structural change would have led because after this short (16-year) period the dynamic of the national immigration debate saw yet another significant shift. Let me explain.

From my point of view it honestly isn't all that hard to see how we got to this hyper-partisan point in the immigration debate. This is to say that in 2016 we had one politician, Trump, running on the slogan "Build the Wall," and the other, Clinton, running on the promise of giving illegal immigrants free healthcare, and this dichotomous split at the top of the proverbial pyramid, as one would expect, eventually made it down to the rest of us. And as a result, the national populace has seemingly followed the political platform positions of these two campaigns and, broadly speaking, one side of the aisle is now staunchly against immigration while the other, at least according to its rhetoric, wants open borders because "No human is illegal." Ergo, when it comes to immigration what could have been a great opportunity to "meet in the middle" instead went the complete opposite direction. I.e., for most of America's history the political elites and the populace alike have been, at the very least close to one another on the issue of immigration; however, since the 2016 election that status quo has fundamentally changed, and probably permanently changed, and as it stands now we live in a political landscape wherein the immigration debate has been reduced down to a simple for/against binary. At any rate, though, that wraps up our brief discussion on the history of immigration in the US.

SIDENOTE

It is a bit hyperbolic to describe the positions of each side of the aisle in the way I did, but again, I was speaking broadly. Anyway, the reality is that the majority of "regular" people on the right have no issue with legal immigration and the majority of "regular" people on the left have no issue with having a border. Of course, with this said, due to political tribalism the actual positions of these two sides are just not extreme enough for our current candidates. This is to say that, as with many things in our modern political landscape, the national immigration debate has left the realm of sanity and, as expected, We the People have followed this race to the extremes. In other words, the way things sit right now, as one side supports a position on immigration, let's say having a strong border, for instance, the other, simply because they do not like that side must go even farther the opposite way. Thus, the inevitable result is that both sides end up going a little too far, and therefore end up in the realm of insanity (i.e., immigration is inherently bad, in all forms, or all immigrants, even illegal immigrants, are the backbone of our nation.). Case in point, perhaps my description of each side's position *is* a bit hyperbolic, but with that said it really isn't that far off. Furthermore, it certainly isn't what each side's positions were just a few years ago.

Alright, so far we have established that the government does, in fact, have the constitutional authority to regulate immigration, as well as what our country has done in the past in regard to that issue. Moving on to the final section of this chapter, given everything that we have talked about thus far, in my summation the United States undoubtedly needs strong borders. This is because strong borders not only allow us to maintain our national security, but equally as important they also allow us to uphold/enforce the immigration standards that We the People have set. Furthermore, and with that said, given what we covered in this chapter I also recognize that we, as a nation, do actually benefit from legal immigration in some fairly significant ways. In other words, even though we absolutely do need to stop the flow of illegal immigrants, at the same time we also need to enhance the flow of legal immigrants.

Now with all of that said, the main issue I see in regard to this issue is that, as things are right now, we have neither of these things. This is to say that illegal immigration is and currently continues to be a problem, as Mayor Adams has recently acknowledged, but at the same time it is very hard to propose sane/reformative immigration/border legislation without half of the country touting you as a racist and a xenophobe. So, what's the solution?

In essence, I believe that the sane position on immigration is to first and foremost do whatever is necessary to secure our borders because this not only allows us to regain control over our immigration process, but it also disincentivizes the Cartels from engaging in their abysmal and horrific human trafficking operations. Furthermore, with this done we will actually begin to increase our country's carrying capacity (how many immigrants we can take on without risking negative economic/social impacts) because by taming the flow of illegal immigrants, which as it stands now is currently overwhelming our immigration system, we will subsequently have more room for *legal* immigrants. Make sense?

Second, when this framework is in place, I believe that we should then begin to revamp legislation like the Immigration and Nationality Act of 1965, but with a few tweaks. Now the reason I say that we should want to do this is that this style of immigration policy, assuming it was reworked to reflect our nation's current employment needs, would turn things over to one of my favorite free market principles, meritocracy. In other words, we would not be focused on specific regions, but rather specific people. Ergo, our country would receive all of the previously mentioned benefits of legal immigration (an influx of highly skilled/highly educated taxpayers, business owners, innovators, etc.) while also not being seen by our western allies as an ethnocentric nation-state that is hyper-focused on its race and/or ethnicity (I know some of you think this is stupid, but international relations are important.).

"But" you ask, "wouldn't this just incentivize more illegal immigration?" Well, first off, our border would be secured by this point if we were approaching this issue from my sane point of view, but regardless, yes, this would still be a concern. Therefore, in order to disincentivize illegal immigration while also being restrictive on who we award citizenship to, I believe a very sane thing to do would be to revamp the Bracero Program. I mean, think about it. If we **1)** have strong borders, **2)** have an unsuppressed legal immigration system, and **3)** have at least some modernized form of the Bracero Program, everybody wins. In other words, if we follow the formula I just laid out, essentially, not only would criminals and terrorists be left unable to enter the country, but in addition to this benefit both highly skilled/educated immigrants and low-skilled/uneducated immigrants alike would be able to easily operate here thus leading to a decrease in illegal immigration and a bolstering of our economy. Oh yeah, and as a third bonus, you know all of those illegal immigrants that we currently have no way of monitoring? Well, in this system even if these types of immigrants weren't awarded outright citizenship they could still work, which means that they won't be incentivized to try and enter illegally, and furthermore we would be able to keep track of them and/or collect taxes. Anyway, to summarize, if our borders are strong and our legal immigration system is reformed, we can quite literally get the best of all worlds (Strict citizenship standards, low levels of illegal immigration, a large pool of low-skilled workers who pay taxes, etc.)

Perhaps this is all a pipe dream and the whole immigration system will continue to spiral between the partisan extremes every 4-8 years while also being bogged down by endless layers of bureaucracy, but nonetheless I strongly believe that We the People can, if we take responsibility over this issue, refrain from migrating (pun intended) to these partisan extremes and can instead push our politicians to enforce sane legislation that would secure our borders, untangle the current legal immigration process, and incentivize low-skilled/uneducated migrants to pursue legal means of coming here that also contribute to the US economy. Well, that's the hope anyway.

Alright, that's it for this one folks. In closing, never forget that my sane position is only a starting point. I mean, I have said it once and I will say it a thousand times before this book is done, but US policymakers, constitutionally speaking, serve the wills and desires of We the People. Therefore my final message to you is to ignore the two extreme positions of the partisans running this country and instead, take what I have told you, do your own follow-on research, and then do what you can as an active citizen to make sure that your sane wills and desires are not only heard, but also acted upon, because if you do, well, then perhaps in the near future immigration will not be such a hot button/divisive issue. Anyway, see you in the next chapter wherein we will be discussing war.

CHAPTER 8

War

The next divisive issue that we are going to discuss in this book is
one that, as a combat veteran, is very near and dear to my heart.
This issue is war and in my view this aspect of humanity is, quite
possibly, the worst thing about our species. Of course, with that said
I am not naïve and I do recognize that sometimes wars are justified
and/or necessary (though very rarely), but still, to be frank I have
personally witnessed the pointlessness of many of our modern wars,
the death and destruction they cause, and the hordes of damaged
individuals, both physically and psychologically, that they leave
behind when they are finished. Ergo, I am not a fan. Anyway, when
I was debating how to go about my research for this chapter, I was
thoroughly stumped on what the best course of action was. I mean,
as a veteran and a political science/psychology professional I thought
that perhaps a good place to start was talking about why we have
wars in the first place, as well as a few examples of what *good* wars
actually look like. However, even though these topics *are* relevant to
a discussion about war, and things that active citizens *should* strive

173

to familiarize themselves with, there is just so much information on these topics that even dipping our toes into the water would quickly send us down a bevy of philosophical rabbit holes and, ultimately, away from our overall goal, finding a sane position on war. Therefore, let me just sum up these two topics, why we have wars in the first place and what a few examples of *good* wars are, by saying first and foremost that all wars, regardless of why they began and/or how they ended, are always a bad thing for humanity.

SIDENOTE

There are many works included in the reference section that cover the reasons nations choose to go to war, and I encourage you to go down these rabbit holes in your own time (A good place to start is Dr. James D. Fearon's article titled *Rationalist Explanations for War*.). The reason for this is that, if you do, then you will quickly see that not only is war extremely *bad* for our species, but also that most of them are rather unnecessary.

Well, you heard it here first folk, yes, even justified wars are, overall, bad for society. This is to say that, for one, all wars end up creating massive economic strains on both the global economy, and the nations actively involved, and this leads to decreased international trade, less local infrastructure development, and last but not least, immense downturns in the investment markets. But more than that, though, they also inherently bring with them the widespread destruction of infrastructure, culture, and human life, which, I think we can all agree is a fairly bad outcome. Furthermore, and the third reason that wars are always a bad thing for society, most wars, and certainly most modern wars, are either illegal, unnecessary, or both, and I say this not because I am a conspiracy theorist, but instead because I have thoroughly studied the academic explanations for war and have found that most wars, especially our wars (Korea, Vietnam, Iraq, Afghanistan, etc.), could have easily been prevented, which in turn means that all of the aforementioned consequences of those wars never needed to happen in the first place. Make sense?

Now even though I strongly believe that all wars are bad, like I said before some wars are still justified and/or necessary. In other words, We the People cannot, as much as I wish we could, simply leave our discussion there. Therefore, in order to find a sane position on war I feel that we need to first figure out what conditions justify going to war and what the US Constitution has to say about this ugly affair. Good to go? Great. To begin, I want to start out by sharing an article I wrote for Wrong Speak Publishing that shows an example of how wars, when we behave in insane ways, can needlessly begin and/or escalate because I think that this will help set the overall tone for this chapter. So, without further to do, let's get into it.

How America Started WWIII
"You Don't Have To Like Putin To Be
Against America's Involvement In His War"

War is ugly and it leaves in its brutal wake not just death and destruction, but also a seemingly endless number of people whose minds and bodies are permanently damaged. Yet, despite these grim aspects of war, the unsavory affair is still quite common within our species and its existence has come to seem, at this point, like an inevitability. The most recent example of this is the bloody war between Russia and Ukraine. The West, and the US in particular, has had a major part to play in the escalation of this war, which is one that could, potentially, spark World War III.

Dr. James Fearon is a political scientist whose work has sought to figure out what causes nations to go to war, and specifically what conditions lead political leaders to prefer war instead of ex-ante (prewar) bargains with competing states. His conclusions are that there are three main reasons that a leader would choose war over diplomacy.

These include one or both nations misinterpreting the strength of the other, a lack of mutual trust, and the existence of incompatible desires, such as one nation wanting to engage in behavior that the other deems to be a human rights violation.

Now, a major factor as to whether or not these conditions have been met depends upon how a leader perceives the international landscape. Since Russia is the explicit aggressor in the Russia/Ukraine conflict what is known about how their leader, Vladimir Putin, sees the current landscape?

Dr. Stephen Benedict Dyson and Dr. Matthew J. Parent, in their academic article entitled *The operational code approach to profiling political leaders: understanding Vladimir Putin* (2017) used a research method known as content analytics to break down Putin's personality structure so that they could determine his psychological patterns, and his underlying behavioral motivations.

The results of this study were that *"Putin holds broadly mainstream beliefs about international politics, albeit qualified by hyper-aggressiveness toward terrorism and a startling preoccupation with political control. His approach is that of an opportunist rather than a strategist."*

Put plainly, Putin may not be the madman we have been led to believe he is but rather is a businessman who is motivated first and foremost by an inherent need for stability. But when Putin feels control slipping, be it due to pressure from outside forces or internally from his own citizens, Putin is more than likely going to resort back to what he knows best, his thuggish nature.

So how does the US factor into this equation?

One of the main drivers of the Russia/Ukraine conflict can be traced back to the US reneging on the 1990 "Iron Clad Guarantees" in which then-Secretary of State James Baker promised Soviet President Mikhail Gorbachev that the US would not expand NATO "one inch farther" to the east of Germany.

Despite making such bold commitments, though, since 1990 three countries [(Estonia, Latvia (2004), and Finland (2023)] that share borders with Russia have been allowed to join NATO, and all of these have done so with the support of the US. Furthermore, Ukraine has received a plethora of support from the US in its attempts to become a part of this organization.

Examples of this support include a 2016 decision by NATO and the US to implement a Comprehensive Assistance Package that provided armed forces support to Ukraine and further assisted their efforts to become a NATO nation, and as recently as 2021 Democratic Senator Chris Murphy stated that once Ukraine received a Membership Action Plan (MAP), a requirement that was just recently removed by NATO, then the next logical step would be for them to join.

But how does all of this influence Putin's decision to invade Ukraine?

As we have seen over the last year and a half Russia is not necessarily the military powerhouse that we thought them to be. Therefore, much like an animal who's wounded and/or weak is going to be hyper-aggressive, Russia's relative lack of military strength might have actually made them less stable than we had previously thought.

So, much like the US does not like enemies moving in on our borders, as evidenced by the Cuban Missile Crisis, an encroaching expansion of NATO to Russia's borders would certainly serve the purpose of making them feel threatened. In addition to this, given our support of post-1990 NATO expansion, the US clearly cannot be trusted when it comes to keeping its word in regard to not allowing Ukraine to join, and this lack of trust is being felt firsthand by a man who craves control and who, when he feels it slipping will likely resort to thuggish behavior.

Therefore, like it or not the US is, in fact, culpable in the hyper-aggressive behavior of Russia. And to make matters worse, since America's leaders do not appear to truly understand the root cause of Putin's actions, much like trying to put out an oil fire with water the more they try to incentivize him to calm down by arming and funding Ukraine, they are actually only fueling the flames of the conflict by increasing his feelings of desperation.

Therefore, it would appear that the goal of US policymakers, instead of increasing tensions with Putin, should actually be to alter Putin's perception of the international landscape so that he no longer sees NATO and the West as an immediate threat. This would allow him to resort back to his normal business-like disposition, thus making him more reasonable and less like a cornered animal.

Or America's leaders could just keep doing what they are doing until this eastern European oil fire eventually blooms into another world war.

As you can see from the example I used in the article (the Russia/Ukraine war), the international landscape can be rather complex, but with that said there are still many ways to avoid starting and/or escalating wars. In this example, for instance, the entire Ukraine war very likely could have been avoided if the West had a better understanding of who Putin is and/or the overall reasons nations go to war in the first place. In lieu of that, though, as I explained we have instead escalated this conflict to a point where, as a nation, we are now not only discussing a possible nuclear war with Russia, but even worse we are still not in any significant way changing course!

*Breathes heavily and tries to avoid letting that mini rant bloom into an all-out anti-war speech.

Ok, rant over. Moving on, since I got that example out of the way and, hopefully, showed you how things in international affairs can easily and unnecessarily spiral out of control, I want to now shift gears and talk about what conditions warrant classifying a war as a "just" war. Before we start, though, let me just start by saying here at the outset that this question is a bit layered, and also depends significantly upon each specific nation's code of morality. I.e., everyone is not operating from the same spectrum of morality and therefore *their* version of right and wrong may be different from ours. Capeesh? Wonderful.

Ok, moving on for real this time, after doing a deep dive into moral philosophy I have come to the conclusion that the only truly just war is one that is done for the explicit purpose of protecting one's own in-group. In other words, a nation is justified in going to war if it does so only for the purpose of protecting its citizens from an explicit outside threat (I.e., if a nation is attacked then it is very clearly just in its decision to defend itself). Of course, with that said this is where things get a bit layered. What I mean by this is that, like I said, most wars, barring actual invasions (or certain situations like stepping in on behalf of the international community to stop explicit human rights violations, genocide, or something akin to those things), can be prevented. And this applies to "just" wars every bit as much as it does "unjust" wars. Ergo, even some "just" wars are still not at all necessary. At any rate, though, with that preface out of the way, let's look at the Russia/Ukraine war and figure out if this war in particular is a "just" war.

SIDENOTE

When it comes to war there isn't really all that much disagreement between the two sides of our political aisle, not on the foundational level that is. This is to say that each side, when it is politically and/or economically beneficial, is more than happy to go to war whether it is justified or not. Therefore, the only *real* friction point between the two sides when it comes to war, at least these days, boils down to what the position of the other team is (i.e., if the Republicans/Democrats are against the war, I am for it!).

Alright, considering the definition I just laid out of what a just war entails, it seems pretty self-evident that in the Russia/Ukraine war Ukraine is clearly justified in its decision to fight. I mean, if fending off a foreign invasion isn't part of protecting one's own in-group (nation) from an explicit outside threat, I don't what is. However, with that said, given the information I covered in my article for Wrong Speak, an argument could also be made that Russia too is engaging in a just war. Now, I know that may sound crazy to some of you and you may even be calling me an agent of Putin as we speak, but hold your horses a minute and hear me out. You see, if the expansion of NATO does, in fact, pose an explicit threat to Russia's sovereignty, and you can certainly make a case that it does, then would it not be an act of defense for Putin to act aggressively? Well, I would still say no (i.e., there were still less-destructive diplomatic solutions available), and I would also point out that, again, very rarely is the juice (bloodshed) of war worth the squeeze (increase in safety), but nonetheless, I can at least see *why* Russia would invade Ukraine, and that *why*, it appears to me, has nothing to do with Putin being the next Adolf Hitler (Let's avoid talking about his war lest we get lumped in with Kayne West). Ergo, yes, Ukraine is justified in its decision to fight, but then again, maybe Russia is as well. Just food for thought, and also an example of how complicated things can get when you are playing the "who's right" game with this issue.

Ok, continuing on with our discussion of war, let's now turn the microscope away from the Russia/Ukraine conflict and instead onto ourselves. In other words, let us now look at two of Americas more recent wars, Vietnam and Iraq, and figure out if these wars were justified. So, beginning with the first of those aforementioned wars, the main justification for the war in Vietnam was, essentially, to stop the spread of communism in Southeast Asia (So that we can stay on track don't get me started on the *real* reasons we got involved in Vietnam.). Now, as a person with Libertarian leanings myself this almost sounds like a just goal because, frankly, I think that communism is utter garbage as a political ideology. With that said, though, I still have to ask, was the spread of communism in Southeast Asia an explicit threat to the safety of the US at that time? Hmmmm, put plainly, the short answer is no, and I say this because, however bad communism truly is, and its bad mind you, to be honest it was/is none of America's business if a country is communist; and it certainly wasn't/isn't explicit enough of a threat to our sovereignty and safety as a nation that stopping its spread in Southeast Asia requires 20 years of war and roughly 1,353,000 lives. Therefore, suffice it to say that the Vietnam war, based on our own definitions, was not a just war. But what about the war in Iraq?

Well, when it comes to the US/Iraq war, a conflict that resulted in yet another 20 odd years of war and hundreds of thousands left dead, unfortunately, this too is an example of an unjustified war. I say this because the official justification for launching this war was that "Saddam Hussein's alleged development of nuclear and biological weapons and purported ties to al-Qaeda made his regime a 'grave and growing' threat to the United States and the world community." Now, again, don't get me started on the *real* reasons for this war, or at least what I believe to be the real reasons behind it, but if we just go off of that official justification, was this war done to explicitly protect the American people? In lay terms, no, it was not. I mean, sure, hindsight is 20/20 and now we know that there weren't actually any weapons of mass destruction (WMDs) in Iraq, but still, for the sake of argument assume there had been. Well, as it stands currently four of the eight nations with nuclear weapons (Russia, China, North Korea, and

Pakistan) are either our enemy, or at the very least not very favorable toward us. Yet, we are not invading their countries and they are not invading ours. Why is this you ask? The answer is simple, mutually assured destruction. In other words, all of these nations know that if they use their nukes, we will use ours too and the whole world ends. Ergo, even though I do not like the idea of Saddam Hussein having nuclear weapons, I have to ask, if this had been the case and he did have nuclear weapons in 2003, would it have been an explicit outside threat to the US citizenry? In my view, no, or at least not any more so than Russia, China, North Korea, and Pakistan all currently having them. Ergo, Iraq, like Vietnam, was also an unjust war.

SIDENOTE

When I have this debate with people they often cite the threat of Iraq gifting WMDs to terrorist organizations. To those people, all I have to say is this. Has the chances of that happening decreased since the Iraq War? I mean, Russia, North Korea, Pakistan, and China all have a ton of nukes and just last week we released 6 billion, previously frozen dollars to Iran. You know them, right? The largest funder of terrorism in the world.... Yep, that's right! Anyway, my point is this. If you think that right now terrorist organizations can't gain access to nuclear weapons, or that the Iraq War in any way lowered their ability to do so, you are not only being naïve, but also denying the scary and unavoidable realities of living in a post-nuclear society.

Alright, so as of right now we have covered most of what I wanted to get to, before moving into what a sane position on war is anyway, but with that said, before getting to my sane position we still need to talk about what the Constitution says about this issue. Let's do that now by looking at Article 1/Section 8 of the US constitution.

US Constitution/ Article 1/Section 8:

- The Congress shall have power to lay and collect taxes, duties, imposts and excises, to pay the debts and provide for the common defense and general welfare of the United States; but all duties, imposts and excises shall be uniform throughout the United States;
- To borrow money on the credit of the United States;
- To regulate commerce with foreign nations, and among the several states, and with the Indian tribes;
- To establish a uniform rule of naturalization, and uniform laws on the subject of bankruptcies throughout the United States;
- To coin money, regulate the value thereof, and of foreign coin, and fix the standard of weights and measures;
- To provide for the punishment of counterfeiting the securities and current coin of the United States;
- To establish post offices and post roads;
- To promote the progress of science and useful arts, by securing for limited times to authors and inventors the exclusive right to their respective writings and discoveries;
- To constitute tribunals inferior to the Supreme Court;
- To define and punish piracies and felonies committed on the high seas, and offenses against the law of nations;
- **To declare war, grant letters of marque and reprisal, and make rules concerning captures on land and water;**
- To raise and support armies, but no appropriation of money to that use shall be for a longer term than two years;

- To provide and maintain a navy;
- To make rules for the government and regulation of the land and naval forces;
- To provide for calling forth the militia to execute the laws of the union, suppress insurrections and repel invasions;
- To provide for organizing, arming, and disciplining, the militia, and for governing such part of them as may be employed in the service of the United States, reserving to the states respectively, the appointment of the officers, and the authority of training the militia according to the discipline prescribed by Congress;
- To exercise exclusive legislation in all cases whatsoever, over such District (not exceeding ten miles square) as may, by cession of particular states, and the acceptance of Congress, become the seat of the government of the United States, and to exercise like authority over all places purchased by the consent of the legislature of the state in which the same shall be, for the erection of forts, magazines, arsenals, dockyards, and other needful buildings; —And
- To make all laws which shall be necessary and proper for carrying into execution the foregoing powers, and all other powers vested by this Constitution in the government of the United States, or in any department or officer thereof.

Hmmm, maybe it was a bit of overkill to list the full section, but to be honest, when it comes to a document that is as important as the US Constitution (and also one that is as tragically underread as the US Constitution), I would rather give you more than is necessary as opposed to giving you, potentially, not enough. Plus, I like the idea of those reading this who have not already read the US Constitution getting some extra albeit inadvertent exposure to it. At any rate, though, for those listening to this book, when I listed Article 1 section 8 of the Constitution, I highlighted in red the portion of it (clause 11) that stated, "To declare war, grant letters of marque and reprisal, and make rules concerning captures on land and water." Now, as I have said before I am not a lawyer who specializes in constitutional law, but this clause seems pretty self-explanatory. This is to say that, put plainly, the US Constitution does, in fact, grant Congress the power to declare war and it does not require any explicit justification for doing so. Make sense?

SIDENOTE

Just as we examined the Vietnam and the Iraq Wars in order to determine if they were "just" wars, look at them again and this time determine for yourself if you think that they were legal wars.

Are you finished? If so, did you come to the realization that these wars, just like all of the wars the US has been in since WWII were illegal wars because Congress never made an official declaration of war in these instances? If you did, move on. If not, reread the last section again and come back to this question.

Ok, are you back? Basically, what you missed the first time was that the Constitution grants *Congress* the power to declare war, not the president. Good to go?

Ok, after briefly reviewing what a "just" war is, as well as what constitutional authority the government has in regard to this unsavory topic, we are finally to the point in the chapter where I tell you what I believe a sane position is on this issue. In essence, I believe that We the People should view the existence of any new war (barring a literal invasion) as an example of our government completely and utterly failing at its job, and we should subsequently let them know it with our voices and our votes. This is because war, as the evidence shows (*Rationalist Explanations for War*), is not only costly in terms of money, infrastructure, and life, but also generally unnecessary. Furthermore, I believe that We the People should not be ok in the least bit with any president, regardless of their partisan alignment, declaring one of these new wars because this would be a clear-cut example of them overstepping their constitutional authority. This is to say that even though this behavior *has* been normalized, at least since the Korean War that is, it simply cannot continue to be the case in a sane society.

Finally, we should, as sane citizens, realize that war is nearly never the answer, and therefore should think beyond our own personal bias's (i.e., I don't like that country's ideology or I don't like that they have that much power) when deciding whether or not to support a war and instead should just look at the situation objectively. Then, and only after that can we attempt to determine if engaging in that war would actually be eliminating an immediate and/or explicit threat; because if it doesn't, well, then you are needlessly supporting murder and destruction on a scale that is so awful that only those of us who have actually been there can truly understand its impact. Anyway, that is what I believe a sane position on war looks like. In lay terms, it's always bad, generally unnecessary, and only Congress should be allowed to declare it.

In closing, if our elected leaders don't share this sane position then, well, by now you already know how to wield our collective power as an active citizenry, don't you? At any rate, that's it for this chapter everyone. See you in the next chapter wherein we will be discussing guns.

CHAPTER 9

Guns

"A well regulated militia, being necessary to the security of a free state, the right of the people to keep and bear arms, ***shall not be infringed***." **(The Second Amendment)**

"The Constitution be never construed to authorize Congress to infringe the just liberty of the press, or the rights of conscience; or to prevent the people of the United States, who are peaceable citizens, from keeping their own arms." **(Samuel Adams)**

"The Second Amendment places no limits on individual ownership of cannon, or any other arms." **(Professor Glen Harlan Reynolds, University of Tennessee)**

"Both [Federalists/Anti-Federalists] believed the greatest danger to the new republic was tyrannical government and that the ultimate check on tyranny was an armed population." **(Professor David Vandercoy, Valparaiso University Law School)**

"Before a standing army can rule, the people must be disarmed; as they are in almost every kingdom of Europe. The supreme power in

189

America cannot enforce unjust laws by the sword; because the whole body of the people are armed, and constitute a force superior to any band of regular troops that can be, on any pretence, raised in the United States." **(Noah Webster)**

"O sir, we should have fine times, indeed, if, to punish tyrants, it were only sufficient to assemble the people! Your arms, wherewith you could defend yourselves, are gone; and you have no longer an aristrocratical, no longer a democratical spirit. Did you ever read of any revolution in a nation, brought about by the punishment of those in power, inflicted by those who had no power at all?" **(Patrick Henry)**

"There is nothing so likely to produce peace as to be well prepared to meet an enemy." **(George Washington)**

"Whenever governments mean to invade the rights and liberties of the people, they always attempt to destroy the militia, in order to raise an army upon their ruins." **(Rep. Elbridge Gerry of Massachusetts)**

"A people who would stand fast in their liberty, should furnish themselves with weapons proper for their defence, and learn the use of them. It is indeed an hard case, that those who are happy in the blessings of providence, and disposed to live peaceably with all men, should be obliged to keep up the idea of blood and slaughter, and expend their time and treasure to acquire the arts and instruments of death. But this is a necessity which the depravity of human nature has laid upon every state. Nor was there ever a people that continued, for any considerable time, in the enjoyment of liberty, who were not in a capacity to defend themselves against invaders, unless they were too poor and inconsiderable to tempt an enemy." **(Simeon Howard)**

"For a people who are free, and who mean to remain so, a well-organized and armed militia is their best security." **(Thomas Jefferson)**

"A militia, when properly formed, are in fact the people themselves... and include all men capable of bearing arms." **(Richard Henry Lee)**

"The supposed quietude of a good man allures the ruffian; while on the other hand, arms like laws discourage and keep the invader and plunderer in awe, and preserve order in the world as well as property. The same balance would be preserved were all the world destitute of arms, for all would be alike; but since some will not, others dare not lay them aside… Horrid mischief would ensue were one half the world deprived of the use of them." **(Thomas Paine)**

"The ultimate authority...resides in the people alone...The advantage of being armed, which the Americans possess over the people of almost every other nation...forms a barrier against the enterprises of ambition." **(James Madison)**

"Are we at last brought to such a humiliating and debasing degradation, that we cannot be trusted with arms for our own defense? Where is the difference between having our arms in our possession and under our own direction, and having them under the management of Congress? If our defense be the real object of having those arms, in whose hands can they be trusted with more propriety, or equal safety to us, as in our own hands?" **(Patrick Henry)**

"None but an armed nation can dispense with a standing army." **(Thomas Jefferson)**

"The militia is the natural defence of a free country against sudden foreign invasions, domestic insurrections and domestic usurpations of power by rulers. It is against sound policy for a free people to keep up large military establishments and standing armies in time of peace both from the enormous expenses with which they are attended and the facile means which they afford to ambitious and unprincipled rulers to subvert the government or trample upon the rights of the people. The right of the citizens to keep and bear arms has justly been considered as the palladium of the liberties of a republic since it offers a strong moral check against the usurpation and arbitrary power of rulers and will generally even if these are successful the first instance enable the people to resist and triumph over them." **(Justice Joseph Story)**

"The great object is, that every man be armed...Every one who is able may have a gun." **(Patrick Henry)**

"The Constitutions of most of our states assert that all power is inherent in the people; that they may exercise it by themselves, in all cases to which they think themselves competent, (as in electing their functionaries executive and legislative, and deciding by a jury of themselves, both fact and law, in all judiciary cases in which any fact is involved) or they may act by representatives, freely and equally chosen; that it is their right and duty to be at all times armed; that they are entitled to freedom of person; freedom of religion; freedom of property; and freedom of the press." **(Thomas Jefferson)**

"The right of self-defense never ceases. It is among the most sacred, and alike necessary to nations and to individuals." **(James Monroe)**

"One man with a gun can control 100 without one." **(Vladimir Lenin)**

Ok, you get the point, I like the Second Amendment. But be that as it may, quotes alone, regardless of how poignant they may or may not be, are not enough in and of themselves to establish a sane position on this chapter's issue. In other words, even though these aforementioned quotes are pretty clear about why our right to bear arms should not be infringed, in order to truly understand this issue it is important that we also give this chapter at least some semblance of nuance and/or contextual depth. Ergo, even though this chapter could, essentially consist of only one sentence, the Second Amendment, I still have a bit more to say. Anyway, the next divisive issue we are going to discuss in this book, as you have probably surmised, is guns, and in order to understand this issue we are actually going to break it down into three subtopics. "Arms," gun control, and crime. Sound like a plan? Great, then without further to do, let's get into it.

To begin, even though I bombarded you with quotes at the outset, I want to share one more that helps explain, in a technical sense, what the term "arms" actually means within the context of the Second Amendment. That quote is as follows:

"It's obvious to the intellectually honest that in using the word 'arms' the Second Amendment's writers acknowledged the right of ordinary citizens to keep and bear the same weapons used by soldiers in the military. Our rights are not and should not be based on the technology at the time those rights were acknowledged."
—TJ Martinell, What Does the Word "Arms" Mean in the 2nd Amendment, June 30th, 2016

Now as always, I would advise checking out this reference in its entirety because it, like the other references I used for this book, is quite informative, but with that said suffice it to say that, as it stands now, We the People have the right to possess any weapon that our standing military has, and this right is very clearly enshrined in our

Constitution. Of course, with that said many people will still disagree with this absolutist perspective, and I would, in some ways, agree with them. I mean, I personally do not think that citizens should be able to casually stroll down to their local gas station and pick up a nuclear weapon, and therefore, despite my love of guns, I myself am not even a true blue Second Amendment absolutist. Be that as it may, though, I also believe that, technically, a scenario like the one I just mentioned should be a real and legal possibility. This is to say that, even I don't actually foresee this reality coming to fruition, until things change (i.e., We the People demand a "no nuke" amendment and/or any other restrictions we would like placed on the 2nd amendment) the law is the law and though shalt not infringe. In other words, all of the gun control arguments coming from the left side of the aisle right now (and the right side as well, looking at you Reagan and Crenshaw) are, at their core, unconstitutional because as it stands currently the "arms" in the Second Amendment, like it or not, means literally any arms. Make sense?

SIDENOTE

Caveat- Weapons of mass destruction (WMDs) are literally the only weapons I want to be restricted. In other words, in *my* America if you want a fighter jet with heat-seeking rockets, I say go nuts! Of course, I also think that background checks are sane and appropriate within the context of that world. I.e., just like with immigration if you don't know who the *who* is you might as well have no due process at all. But with that said, my overall point still stands. This is to say that, after it *has* been confirmed that you are a US citizen over the age of 18, constitutionally speaking the government really has no business telling you that you are not allowed to have a fighter jet because if we are going by our own Constitution, put plainly, buying that jet is one of your inherent rights as an American citizen. Ergo, if you have the money for it, enjoy.

P.S. With all of that said, a private seller can still make their own determination about your mental fitness and decide not to sell you the jet, so, there are, technically, still checks and balances in this version of America, they are just coming from the free market, not the government. Anyway, let's move on.

Ok, so the "arms" in the Second Amendment, technically speaking, means pretty much everything, at least right now. Well, even though I can't change that reality, nor would I want to, I still want to spend the last part of this brief chapter explaining some silver linings to you, or at least to those of you who aren't big fans of guns, because this world I just outlined, even though we can't change it (not without a new Amendment that is) is actually not as scary as it sounds. Let me explain.

SIDENOTE

The Second Amendment was never about hunting or target shooting. It is about defending against enemies foreign and domestic. Now, as a military tactician with on-the-ground experience, I want to explain something to all of you (especially to my pro-gun readers/listeners). In lay terms, if you think that a bunch of citizens simply having a healthy stockpile of weapons will stop an enemy, foreign or domestic, then you are out of touch with reality. This is to say that if you are a pro-Second Amendment guy/girl what you actually need to be focusing on is the "well-regulated militia" portion of the Second Amendment, not the "bearing arms portion," and I say this because this is the actual meat and potatoes of that beautiful amendment, even though it does not get nearly enough attention (Looking at you, my fellow gun people!). I digress though.

In sum, organize, train, and take your responsibilities as an active citizen seriously. I.e., don't just sit alone in your bunker waiting for the feds to hit your booby traps because, as a nation, if we do have to fend off a tyrant, in the grand scheme of thing a bunch of isolated, Waco-style instances of violence will, essentially, be pointless and ineffective. Ergo, if you care about defending against tyranny, which is the actual purpose of the Second Amendment, then you should also start caring about the full Second Amendment (the "well-regulated militia" portion), and not just the part that's easy (buying cool guns). Good to go?

P.S. To the FBI agent reading this, I am not an extremist. Rather, I am a patriot who loves liberty and understand that it can always be taken away if We the People lose our constitutionally enshrined right to defend ourselves. So, please do not send me to the Gulag.

Alright, so in essence the silver lining of having a constitution with such a permissive Second Amendment is that, put plainly, more guns actually lead to less violence and less tyranny. This is to say that, as counterintuitive as it may sound, an armed society is a polite society, and the statistics bear this out (check out the references if you don't believe me). You see, just like we never have nuclear war because of mutually assured destruction, on the micro-level people are much less likely to engage in violence if they know that the person they are "beefing" with is armed as well (Non-sidenote sidenote, this is actually why 98% of mass shootings occur in gun-free zones. I.e., gun free zones are what is known as "soft targets," which is a military term that is used to describe a target that is weak and/or poorly defended.). More than this, though, a well-armed population also disincentivizes tyranny because, along the same line as the aforementioned Lenin quote, one man with a gun (a government with tyrannical ambitions) cannot control one hundred men who also have guns (We the People). Ergo, the more legal gun owners you have the less violence and/or tyranny you have? Got it?

SIDENOTE

If I could snap my fingers and make all of the guns everywhere disappear, I might just do it. Ok, probably not because guns have, for the first time ever in human history given women, the elderly, the weak, and the disabled the ability to defend themselves, but my point is that I get the logic behind that position. Regardless of what I would do, though, this is simply not a feasible goal. This is to say that in a nation, like America for instance, that right now has over 393 million privately owned guns circulating within its population, the idea that you could ever truly remove all the guns is a farce. Furthermore, as Second Amendment advocate and famous author Dr. John R. Lott Jr. said, even if you *were* to somehow remove all of America's guns…. how long until all of those guns just came back in through the border? Just food for thought.

Ok folks, we are almost done so bear with me. In this chapter we have discussed what "arms" We the People are constitutionally authorized to have, how any and all restrictions on these arms, from a legal perspective, are unconstitutional, and also that this is not necessarily a bad thing, despite how it sounds. Well, with all of that out of the way it is now time to, as we do at the end of every chapter, establish a sane position on the issue we have been discussing. To begin, put frankly "what is sane" is somewhat irrelevant when it comes to the issue of guns because, as I have pointed out many times thus far, the Constitution is pretty clear on this topic. But be that as it may, since I know that many of the anti-gun and anti-gun adjacent readers/listeners will still not be pleased with this assessment, let me just say that if you would prefer a more restrictive Constitution instead of the one we have now, at least when it comes to guns that is, you can do so in the same way you would change anything else about our Constitution. I.e., you do have the ability to alter this constitutional status quo by wielding your power as an active citizenry (Although I would prefer you didn't!). With that said, though, before you do this just take into consideration what our country would look like if our population *was* actually disarmed, or at least disarmed to the point where we posed no real threat to the US government. In other words, do you really have faith that no one in our government will ever become tyrannical? Maybe you do, and if that is the case so be it, but as for me, I personally do not, and that is why, like the founding fathers, I believe that the 2nd amendment, even with all of its widespread and sometimes seemingly insane permissions, is overall a very sane piece of legislation.

At any rate, putting aside the legal/Constitutional ramifications of this debate, the sane position on guns is that maintaining our right to have them is very important because without this right, to put it lightly, we don't have any of our rights. This is to say that should the government ever decide to infringe upon one of We the Peoples liberties, like free speech, for instance, as unpleasant as it is to think about guns and well-regulated militias *will* be our only recourse. Furthermore, given this fact it is also sane to believe that our gun rights should not be limited to "hunting rifles" and/or guns used for "sport shooting," and the reason for this, again, is because the point of having guns in the first place is so that We the People have the ability to fight. In other words, the only way we can realistically use guns to defend our liberties is by having access to the very same guns that will be used against us (I.e., the government's vast collection of "weapons of war."). And last but not least, without taking into consideration the fact that removing America's guns would be, in essence a "fool's errand," as the data shows (read *More Guns Less Crime* by Dr. Lott) a well-armed society is a polite one. Ergo, it is not insane, but rather a quantitative fact that as the number of law-abiding gun owners increases in our country, the amount of violence, crime, and victimization decreases.

Ok folks, that's it for this chapter. In closing, I know it was a short one, but I hope you still got something out of it. Either way, though, goodbye for now and I will see you in the next one wherein we will be talking about welfare, homelessness, mental illness, and addiction.

CLOSING SIDENOTE

As you may well have noticed, in this chapter I did not discuss where the two sides of the aisle disagree on this topic. The reason for this is that the US Constitution is fairly unambiguous on the topic of guns, so any disagreement between the two sides should be easily remedied. Well, that and because, to be honest the politicians on both sides dislike guns. I mean, sure, the right-wing politicians will *say* they like your guns, but just like they say they love Jesus, this is only to get your vote. In other words, the politicians on the right side of the aisle, broadly speaking, do not want to have to fear We the People any more than those on the left do. Ergo, they, like all politicians, are more than happy to let you have guns, but only to the extent that you are not a threat, which, again, defeats the whole purpose of the Second Amendment in the first place. Anyway, I just wanted to let you know why that topic was not addressed. In sum, both sides of the aisle agree that your right to keep and bear arms *should* be infringed, though to differing degrees, and therefore, when it comes to guns at least, both of the sides are, constitutionally speaking, insane.

CHAPTER 10

Welfare, Homelessness, Mental Illness, And Addiction

As the name of this chapter suggests, in it we will be simultaneously discussing not one, but several different divisive issues. Now the reason I made this decision, combining these issues that is, is because they are actually all somewhat related (I know, big shock, right?). Furthermore, they all, in essence, stem from the same constitutional question. This is to say that all of these issues, in some form or another, beg the question, "What is the government's role in aiding those who have failed to achieve life, liberty, and the ownership of property on their own?" Good to go? Very well, then let's dive in, shall we?

So, when I say welfare I am talking about much more than just Section Eight housing and WIC. Sure, these are microcosms of welfare, but when I use this term I am specifically referencing the framework of our social safety net system as a whole. In other words, every single government program that uses taxpayer dollars to help those who either can't or won't help themselves. Therefore, my starting point for this issue, in lieu of going into the history of welfare, is instead going to be establishing whether or not the federal government even has a role in the welfare game, or if it should just butt out entirely (If it is the latter then I imagine this will be a rather short chapter, aye?).

SIDENOTE

When it comes to these issues neither the left side of the aisle nor the right side of the aisle deny that they are a major problem. In other words, the main point of disagreement is not whether there is a problem, but rather how to solve it. I.e., the right wants strict and swift action taken to "clean" the streets while the left wants to provide "aid" so that the people affected by these issues can get back on their feet. Good to go?

To begin, I want to first share with you Article One, Section Eight, Clause One of the US Constitution because this is the portion of that Constitution that forms the bedrock of the pro-welfare position, and therefore is something that you should be aware of.

Article 1/Section 8/Clause 1:

"The Congress shall have Power To lay and collect Taxes, Duties, Imposts and Excises, to pay the Debts and provide for the common Defence and general Welfare of the United States;"

Now, at face value this clause suggests that welfare is, in fact, very much the business of the federal government. However, if we take into account the context of when this document was written, that is actually not what it says at all, and to help explain this I want to share part of an article written by Paul Engel, who, among other things is a subject matter expert on the US Constitution. That excerpt, which is pulled from Engel's article entitled *General Welfare Clause* is as follows:

There are several phrases in the Constitution that are regularly misrepresented. One of the most common is Congress's power to provide for the "general welfare" of the United States. So let's break down that phrase so we can understand it.

GEN'ERAL: Public; common; relating to or comprehending the whole community; as the general interest or safety of a nation.

WELFARE: Exemption from any unusual evil or calamity; the enjoyment of peace and prosperity, or the ordinary blessings of society and civil government; applied to states.

—Websters 1828 Dictionary

So, general welfare, when applied to the states, means the exemption from unusual evil or calamity and the enjoyment of peace, prosperity, and blessings of society for the community as a whole. The next logical question should be, "What community?"

Notice the Constitution does not say the general welfare of the people of the United States, nor the general welfare of the States, but of the United States. Today, when we think of the United States, we usually think of a nation broken into 50 subdivisions we call states, but when the Constitution was ratified, we had 13 independent states who joined together and delegated some of their powers to a central government called the United States. This distinction may seem trivial, but it is actually quite important. If the United States is a single government subdivided into smaller units we call states, then Washington rules and your states are really colonies of

Washington, not much different than their condition in 1776 under British rule. If, however, we are 50 sovereign states who have delegated some of their power to the union, and if the term United States refers to the union and its central government, then the meaning of the phrase, "The Congress shall have Power To lay and collect Taxes, Duties, Imposts and Excises, to pay the Debts and provide for the common Defense and general Welfare of the United States" means something different. It means that Congress can collect taxes to pay the debts of the federal government, not those of the states. It means Congress can collect taxes to pay for the defense of the nation as a whole, not the defense of individual states. And most importantly, it means Congress can collect taxes to pay for the general welfare of the United States, not the people or the individual states.

I know this is not what we've been taught, and you may be thinking that I'm pulling this out of thin air. Actually I looked to the words of James Madison, known as the "Father of the Constitution", when he was debating the Cod Fisheries bill in the House of Representatives in February 1792. The bill in question included a provision for the central government to provide bounties to cod fisherman as a way to encourage people to join the profession. During the debate, on February 3rd, Mr. Giles said:

"The present section of the bill (he continued) appears to contain a direct bounty on occupations; and if that be its object, it is the first attempt as yet made by this government to exercise such authority; — and its constitutionality struck him in a doubtful point of view; for in no part of the

Constitution could he, in express terms, find a power given to Congress to grant bounties on occupations: the power is neither {427} directly granted, nor (by any reasonable construction that he could give) annexed to any other specified in the Constitution."

—Debate on the On the Cod Fishery Bill, granting Bounties, House of Representatives, February 3, 1792

No one, not even those who supported the bill, could come up with any reasonable way of showing that the Constitution gave Congress this power. Later, on February 7th, Mr. Madison went into a detailed explanation of why the common defense and general welfare clauses could not be used to justify Congress having the power to spend money in that way.

"It is to be recollected that the terms "common defence and general welfare," as here used, are not novel terms, first introduced into this Constitution. They are terms familiar in their construction, and well known to the people of America. They are repeatedly found in the old Articles of Confederation, where, although they are susceptible of as great a latitude as can be given them by the context here, it was never supposed or pretended that they conveyed any such power as is now assigned to them. On the contrary, it was always considered clear and certain that the old Congress was limited to the enumerated powers, and that the enumeration limited and explained the general terms."

—Debate on the On the Cod Fishery Bill, granting Bounties, House of Representatives, February 3, 1792

In short, never before had it been considered that Congress would have the power to collect taxes to be used for anything it thought was good or for the general welfare. Mr. Madison went on to describe the dangers of granting Congress such power.

> *"If Congress can employ money indefinitely to the general welfare, and are the sole and supreme judges of the general welfare, they may take the care of religion into their Own hands; they may a point teachers in every state, county, and parish, and pay them out of their public treasury; they may take into their own hands the education of children, establishing in like manner schools throughout the Union; they may assume the provision for the poor; they may undertake the regulation of all roads other than post-roads; in short, every thing, from the highest object of state legislation down to the most minute object of police, would be thrown under the power of Congress; for every object I have mentioned would admit of the application of money, and might be called, if Congress pleased, provisions for the general welfare."*

—Debate on the On the Cod Fishery Bill, granting Bounties, House of Representatives, February 3, 1792

Mr. Madison recognized that if we gave Congress the power to determine what is and is not for the general welfare of the United States, then every portion of your life would be under the control of Congress. As we see today, Congress has inserted itself into education, traffic laws, and even state and local law enforcement. While I did not mention religion as Mr. Madison has, it is only because Congress has abdicated their responsibility to oversee the courts, who have taken care to arbitrate religious views. Because Congress routinely delegates their powers to the executive and judicial branches, we now live in a nation where literally everything is a federal case.

"In short, sir, without going farther into the subject. Which I should not have here touched at all but for the reasons already mentioned, I venture to declare it as my opinion, that, were the power of Congress to be established in the latitude contended for, it would subvert the very foundations, and transmute the very nature of the limited government established by the people of America; and what inferences might be drawn, or what consequences ensue, from such a step, it is incumbent on us all to consider."

—Debate on the On the Cod Fishery Bill, granting Bounties, House of Representatives, February 3, 1792

Mr. Madison was right. As we have seen through history, Congress' appetite for control over the citizenry has grown without limit or restraint. The very idea that there are limitations on the federal government is all but heresy in today's political and judicial environments. No limitations exist on Congress but what the supreme Court bothers to decree and the role of the states is no longer even considered. I wish previous generations had bothered to consider the consequences of giving Congress power beyond their constitutional boundaries and can only encourage that we today not only consider them, but begin enforcing those boundaries again.

So as you can see, despite the seemingly self-evident language that the aforementioned clause touts, welfare is, in fact, not something that the Constitution grants Congress the power to manage. Of course, this does not mean that the states themselves cannot enact welfare policies, but still, as Engel says, this power does not apply to the federal government.

Now I suppose that, in a technical sense, we could just end our discussion here. In other words, since the federal government doesn't actually have any authority over the welfare state to begin with, there is really no need to discuss a sane position in regard to their involvement. But with that said, though, much like the issue of marriage, whether they should or should not be involved in the issue of welfare, they are. And furthermore, they also appear to show no interest, as is generally the case, in relinquishing this power. Ergo, because we do not live in some Libertarian fantasy land, I want to continue on. This is to say that, since the federal government *is* involved in the welfare game, and likely will be until We the People decide otherwise, I want to still try and establish at least a few sane ways that they can be involved (Though I would much prefer we take this power from them!). Sound like a plan? Great.

SIDENOTE

It is worth pointing out that the welfare state possesses a similar flaw to the environmentalism regime. This is to say that, for the most part, unelected bureaucrats are running the show when it comes to the welfare state, and these people, unlike elected officials, are not people beholden to We the People. Ergo, We the People should demand a change to this and require that the people running the welfare state be able to be replaced.

Ok, so assuming that the federal government *will* produce/manage welfare programs, what should these programs actually look like? Well, since this is a rather broad question, to make our conclusion a bit more understandable, in lieu of trying to answer it all in one go let's instead break into 2 separate questions. First, what should financial aid programs in particular look like, and second, what should homelessness care look like.

SIDENOTE

I broke that question into two parts because, in my view, these are the two main dimensions of the welfare debate. So, if we find sane answers for these two questions independently of one another, then, put plainly we will be able to more easily find a sane position on the issue of welfare as a whole. Capeesh?

Alright, so the first question we need to answer is "what should financial aid programs look like." Well, in my summation the crux of the issue here is the goal of the program. In other words, does the program promote permanent dependency, or is it simply a temporary means of getting someone back on their own two feet. Now as you may have guessed, given my Libertarian roots and all, I firmly line up on the latter side of this question. This is to say that I think the goal of any welfare program that grants financial aid to citizens should be centered around getting people back to a place where they can support themselves on their own, not on fostering lifelong dependency. Well, unfortunately this is not the case and, in fact, most of our financial aid programs not only allow people to become permanently dependent upon them, but they also encourage it. To explain this, let me give you a personal example, which, yes, is anecdotal, but also highly reflective of my overall point (If you do not believe me look up the programs yourself. All of their requirements/descriptions are all accessible to the public at https://www.usa.gov/benefits.).

To begin, growing up I knew a woman named, well, I don't want to dox anyone so we will call her Sandy. Well, as fate would have it Sandy had an abusive alcoholic husband who could not only not hold down a job, but who also had his legs amputated because of late-stage diabetes. Now as you can imagine, this unfortunate turn of events put a tremendous financial strain on Sandy, as well as her two children. Nonetheless, though, she plowed forward working two jobs and doing everything in her power to keep the lights on and her kids fed.

Well, as hard as she worked it still wasn't enough for Sandy to make ends meet, especially because she had recently inherited half of her soon-to-be ex-husband's medical bills. So, what does Sandy do, she goes down to the local welfare office and tells them that that she needs a little assistance. Now one would assume that a single mother working two jobs would be at the top of the list for people getting financial aid, right? Wrong, in fact, Sandy was told that not only could they not help her, but also that in order to receive help she needed to quit not one of her jobs, but both.

Now I know that was an anecdotal example, but like I said, if you don't believe me look up these programs for yourself because, if you do, then you will find that most of them follow similar guidelines. Furthermore, you will also see that, even though *some* of them require proof that you are looking for work, these standards are often as simple as meeting once a month with a social worker (now via telehealth) who asks you how the job search is going. I.e., they will not ask for proof of your job search, they only want to connect with you to ensure that you still "need" the assistance.

So, with that insane example in mind, what is a sane version of these programs? Well, in my view it is actually very simple. First, there should be a stringent timeframe enforced with each program, as well as a waiting period in between uses of that program. In other words, much like the way normal unemployment works, from the get-go there should be a specific beginning date, and more importantly, a specific end date because this removes the possibility of becoming dependent on these programs in the long term. Furthermore, if you do have to use one of these programs then you should not be able to simply "restart" that program. Rather, you should have to wait and requalify for that program again later. This is to say that, instead of the current status quo, in which a person can just continue to "renew" their membership in a financial aid program indefinitely, welfare recipients in my sane America would have to prove that they still need the assistance every time that program ended. And they would also have to wait a bit to apply as well. I.e., if you could not prove that you still needed the program, after your mandatory waiting period that is, then, put frankly, you would not be able to use it anymore.

Second, and this one will help ensure that the first one is not abused, there should be a lifetime cap on the overall number of benefits you are allowed to use, as well as an incentive to use only what you need. This is to say that there should be an overall dollar amount that each citizen is entitled to, and this dollar amount covers all of the individual programs (i.e., if you use $5,000 from one program and $3,000 from another program, you have cut your lifetime allotment by $8,000.). Furthermore, given this lifetime cap citizens should have the ability to accept only what they need, not what is available. For instance, if I recently lost my job and am having to dip into my savings while I look for work, because I do not know how long it will take to find a new job, or if I will need to use a welfare program again in the future, I may stretch my financial aid out with smaller payments instead of taking the full amount I actually qualify for. In other words, I simply use the amount of welfare needed to "get me by" at the time, thus allowing me to keep some aid available if I experience financial difficulties again in the future (This will also incentivize people abusing the system to get off their ass and look for work!). Anyway, that is what a sane financial aid system looks like, at least to me.

SIDENOTE

It should go without saying that in this system people will not be penalized for having jobs and they will, more importantly, not be rewarded for having children. In other words, given the lifetime cap on benefits, and the fact that someone cannot become permanently reliant on this system, it should be rather self-regulating. Ergo, in lieu of a subpar qualification process wherein once you are accepted you can quit your job and get an endless supply of dough that increases with every child, this system would instead put the responsibility back on the citizen, thus forcing *them* to be the ones to get their life back in order, and not the taxpayer.

P.S. Obviously exceptions will be given to those who are physically disabled. I.e., the physically disabled should be taken care of indefinitely because they really have no choice in the matter.

Now before moving on to homelessness, let me just say that I know some people will think that I should add a third requirement to this system. This is to say that many people would like the people on financial aid programs to also provide proof that they are looking for work; and I get that, but to be honest I don't trust the "checkers" of this proof, and neither should you (To be honest I don't trust the people figuring out who qualifies for these programs either, but what are you going to do?). Besides, whether you trust them or not, the work thing, under my sane system, would be essentially irrelevant.

You see, if people have a lifetime cap on their benefits, as well as a waiting period between using programs, well, then they really have no choice but to get off the programs at some point, don't they? At any rate, in sum I think that this sane system would allow the people who actually need help to get it, while also forcing those who are abusing the system, at some point, to go their own way. Make sense?

SIDENOTE

Social security is often lumped in with the other welfare programs, likely because it helps make the numbers look a little more palatable, but I did not do this, and the reason for that is because, in theory, we all pay into social security with our taxes. Ergo, it is, in essence, a mandatory government retirement program, albeit one that is failing and will likely not exist soon, that we all fund with our tax dollars, not a welfare program wherein we get something for nothing.

Ok, moving on to the second question, "what should homelessness care look like?" So, the way I see it is that this question involves two main facets, mental illness, and addiction. This is to say that these two issues are, in essence, the reason we have a homelessness crisis in the first place (the housing market doesn't help either, but I'm not going to get into that here); and the reason I say this is because not only have I myself done a lot of research on this topic during my time in grad school and found this to be the case, but also because, according to the medical commmunity "two-thirds of surveyed homeless adults in the U.S. have a mental health and/or substance use disorder." Now this is a rather significant number given that only one in nine Americans, on average, suffer from a substance abuse disorder, and only 4-6%

suffer from a serious mental disorder, is it not? Ergo, and case in point, these problems correlate heavily with the homeless community, which as of 2020 was over five hundred thousand strong, and therefore, if we can solve these then we will also, by proxy, solve the majority of homelessness. Of course, solving these issues is still no easy feat, but it does help to look at them separately, so let's do that now.

Beginning with severe mental illness, technically this problem was pretty much already solved before the civil rights era. This is to say that before the civil right era homelessness, though still a problem, was primarily confined to compact urban areas, such as Skid Row for instance. However, during the civil rights movement the fight for deinstitutionalization (shutting down looney bins) came to full term and with this maturing agenda hundreds of psychiatric institutions were subsequently shut down. And the result was that tens of thousands of mentally ill people were left to roam the streets. Now, I obviously recognize that there were significant issues with many of these institutions, such as the world famous Willowbrook State School facility that was exposed in 1972 for engaging in heinous human rights violations; but nonetheless I think that it was still a mistake throwing the baby out with the bathwater in this scenario because after institutions like Willowbrook were closed it didn't take long (about eight years) before the homeless population in the US had increased to roughly 300,000, a number that dwarfed the per-city statistics from the 1960s and 1970s.

At any rate, though, to solve the mental health aspect of homelessness, I believe that the current data supports the idea that it would be a very sane idea to bring back these mental institutions, albeit with stricter oversight and/or standards of care, because this would, essentially, give all of those mentally ill homeless people a path toward recovery.

In other words, in lieu of letting severely mentally ill people try and survive on their own, which, to be frank is a hazard to both them and us, we should instead get them the help they need. Anyway, let's move on to addiction because that too has a rather simple and sane answer.

SIDENOTE

An important caveat I want to bring up is the danger of mandatory institutionalization. This is to say that the last thing sane citizens need is for the government to have yet another excuse to remove their constitutional rights, am I **right**? Yeah, I know, that joke sucked…. At any rate, just keep in mind that this institutionalization would only apply to the homeless, and ONLY if they were a public nuisance/safety hazard. I.e., if you are out of your mind in your own home, tell the government to screw off, however, if you are sleeping outside of the local Walmart in a puddle of your own vomit, well, then you are a problem for all of us and therefore are subject to being institutionalized.

Second, this institutionalization, like my financial aid programs, is not designed to be permanent. In other words, just like how only the physically disabled get permanent/indefinite financial aid, only the mentally disabled should be permanently/indefinitely institutionalized. The others, whatever that percentage may be, should, to the best of that institution's ability be treated and then reintegrated into society.

Alright, so, addiction. To begin, yes, like mental illness this facet of the homelessness problem has a fairly clear cut answer as well, but with that said it is also one that is not quite as effective as the answer for mental illness was. What I mean by that is that, essentially, unlike mental illness you cannot treat someone for addiction who doesn't want to be treated. In other words, and speaking as a recovered addict myself here, if someone doesn't want to get clean, they won't. Anyway, when it comes to this aspect of the homelessness issue, in my view the sanest way possible to handle this issue is to establish mandatory rehab programs for these people. I.e., if a person is addicted to heroin and sleeping outside your local Walmart, well, then they are, again, a problem for all of us, and therefore we have every right to make them get clean. Of course, with that said, and this is why I said this solution isn't as effective as the mental illness one, if you know anything about rehab programs then you know that their success rate is only about 30 percent (less than one-third). Ergo, this may not be a long-term solution that *truly* solves the problem; but then again, there is only so much we can do for these people in the first place. At any rate, from my perspective giving these people treatment, even if it isn't a permanent solution, is still far better and far saner than simply jailing them, which is only treating the symptoms, not the issue itself.

SIDENOTE

If someone has repeatedly been to rehab but continues to be homeless because of their addiction anyway, well, then frankly put thems the breaks kid. In other words, if a person refuses to stand on their two feet even after repeated treatment, then we will need to either incarcerate them so that they are not disturbing/putting at risk the public, or we will need to enroll them in a long-term care facility, like, for instance, a mental institution. But again, this is only if they continue to be a problem for all of us. I.e., if they do make it through treatment and then they want to consume drugs/alcohol on their own time, though

I would advise against it, that's none of my concern, or yours for that matter. Ergo, this "sane solution" only applies to people who have made their problem everybody's problem. Make sense?

Ok, so now that we have broken down both parts of the homelessness problem individually, I think that we are finally ready to establish a sane position on welfare as a whole. So, without further to do, let's get into it. First and foremost, let me just say that technically the federal government has no constitutional authority to create/fund welfare programs and therefore, constitutionally speaking, it should be exclusively a states' issue. But be that as it may, the government is, in fact, involved in the welfare state, and furthermore it shows no signs of relinquishing this power, at least not any time soon that is. Ergo, at the end of the day this sane position on welfare is, in essence, the best of a bad situation (We the People can change this though!). Good to go? Sweet.

SIDENOTE

To reiterate, though elected officials allocate welfare spending, they are not the ones primarily responsible for guiding that money. Ergo, just like with the EPA, We the People should have a say over who is making/managing the existing welfare programs, as well as the ones that are yet to come.

Alright, the sane citizens position on welfare is that, first, the people running welfare should be elected officials, not unelected bureaucrats, because anyone who is directly involved in spending our money should be beholden to We the People, not the current administration. Second, each and every citizen on welfare, with the exception of the disabled, should have a lifetime cap when it comes to the amount of aid they can receive that cannot be adjusted. Furthermore, they should also be incentivized, through program waiting periods and/or this lifetime cap, to find long-term, non-government solutions for their economic hardships (i.e., getting a job, working with a private sector charity, etc.) because, if this is done, then the new system, unlike its predecessor, will contain an inherent ability to self-regulate, thus removing the ability of users to become permanently dependent on it. Still with me? Awesome.

Third, when it comes to welfare programs/spending for the homeless, in my view we should first and foremost revamp the mental institution framework/infrastructure so that those who are homeless due to mental illness can be removed from the streets and rehabilitated/cared for in a safe and comfortable environment. Furthermore, and in addition to this aforementioned policy, mandatory short-term/long-term rehab should be implemented for those who are homeless specifically due to substance abuse, with the caveat, of course, that repeat offenders will eventually be subject to imprisonment and/or long-term care in a medical facility, like, for instance, a mental institution. Anyway, to summarize, if both of these measures are implemented/enforced, it is reasonable to predict a decrease in homelessness that is upward of 60-70 percent. Ergo, if these positions are enforced we will, in essence, solve the homelessness crisis.

Alright everyone, that is my sane position on welfare, homelessness, mental illness, and addiction. In closing, I know that it might not be a perfect solution, but given the scope of the problem, as well as how limited the government is when it comes to solving that problem (which I would rather have than a less-restricted government mind you) I think that it is still a very reasonable starting place. Anyway,

I hope you enjoyed the chapter, even if you disagreed with some/all of it, but either way, it is now time to move on to the next chapter, our final chapter, wherein I will bringing this whole thing to an end.

CHAPTER 11

Conclusion

Well friends, it's been real but I think it is finally time to go. But before I do, though, I just have a few things to say. First, we live in an unbelievably vast, and I would argue corrupt bureaucracy. This is to say that what was supposed to be a government for the people by the people has instead turned into a massive leviathan of corruption, political favors, special interest groups, controlled opposition, and cronyism. Frankly, and I am just being honest here, this is a pitiful status quo for a nation that, in theory and practice, is supposed to represent a nation run on the premise that We the People hold inherent power over the nation-state. But with that said, though, I do still have hope for our future because, as I have said many times in these pages, this does not *have* to be the case. In other words, We the People, if we were to so choose, could still regain the reigns of political power in the US and set things right. Of course, this is easier said than done, but nonetheless, I think that we can do it. So, in light of these grim aforementioned facts, I implore all of you to become active citizens and to start looking at the political landscape as a battleground of ideas, not of political parties, because if you don't this once great nation will only continue to crumble, crushing all of us under its demise.

Second, you may have disagreed with some of the sane positions I outlined in this book. Hell, you may have disagreed with all of them. But be that as it may, I hope that they still, at the very least, showed you that all too often neither side has everything completely right. This is to say that, just like no one person will have all of the right answers, neither will any one specific political faction. Furthermore, even if you did find yourself disagreeing with my sane positions, I hope that this book helped explain to you that neither party, not even the Republican party, care all that much about our founding documents. In other words, if you are so deeply ensconced in the political tribalism that has ravaged our nation that you believe *your* party is fighting for individual liberty, I hope that this book, if nothing else, opened your eyes to the reality that both sides, depending on the situation, are more than happy to trample your constitutional rights if it aids their political agenda.

Third, for all of the political newcomers out there, don't let this book be the be all and end all of your search for sane positions. Rather, look at it as a jumping off point and use my method of finding the root source of disagreement on each issue to enlighten your own journey to becoming a political sophisticate.

Fourth, and this is the final thing I want to say, never forget that We the People are bound by duty to make sure our elected officials are upholding the ideals of the US Constitution, which is a document centered around individual liberty and We the People's inherent power over the government. In other words, politicians spend billions of dollars each year trying to find out how you feel. Ergo, there is no good reason why we as active citizens cannot make our voices heard and influence our elected leaders to uphold these principles as well. So, organize events, vote with purpose, and/or even write your elected leaders so that We the People can, together, undo this corrupt system and return it to a sane and constitutional status quo.

Alright folks. I believe that's it. In closing, never forget that this country is only as strong as our will to maintain it. So, put plainly, get off the couch, stop being a passive citizen, and start helping me return this country to sanity.

References .... For the Nerds

P.S. Each of these references have references of their own. Ergo, if you do not find what you are looking for in the initial source…. keep digging.

Chapter 1: Introduction

Aristotle. (2017). Politics. Hackett Publishing Company, Inc. (Original work published 350 B.C.E.)

Benoit, K. (2006). Duverger's Law and the Study of Electoral Systems. *French Politics*, 4(1), 69–83. https://doi.org/10.1057/palgrave.fp.8200092

Likitkijsomboon, P. (1992). The Hegelian dialectic and Marx's "Capital." Cambridge Journal of Economics, 16(4), 405–419. https://www.jstor.org/stable/23599623

Maybee, J. F. (2016). Hegel's Dialectics (Stanford Encyclopedia of Philosophy). Stanford.edu. https://plato.stanford.edu/entries/hegel-dialectics/

Philip E. Converse (2006) The nature of belief systems in mass publics (1964), Critical Review, 18:1-3, 1-74, DOI: 10.1080/08913810608443650

Riker, W. H. (1982). The Two-Party System and Duverger's Law: An Essay on the History of Political Science. *The American Political Science Review*, 76(4), 753. https://doi.org/10.2307/1962968

Roberts, S. (2015, January 8). Prof. Philip E. Converse, Expert on How Voters Decide, Dies at 86. The New York Times. https://www.nytimes.com/2015/01/08/us/prof-philip-e-converse-86-expert-on-how-voters-decide.html

Chapter 2: Partisanship

Desan, S. (2011). Internationalizing the French Revolution. French Politics, Culture & Society. https://www.jstor.org/stable/42843715

Dobell, W. M. (1986). Updating Duverger's Law. Canadian Journal of Political Science. https://www.jstor.org/stable/3227706

Editors of Connect Us. (2019, July 14). 16 Major Pros and Cons of the Two Party System in America. ConnectUS.com. https://connectusfund. org/16-major-pros-and-cons-of-the-two-party-system-in-america

Erikson, R. S., Wright, G. C., & McIver, J. P. (1989). Political Parties, Public Opinion, and State Policy in the United States. American Political Science Review, 83(3), 729–750. https://doi. org/10.2307/1962058

Feinstein, Y. (2019). Nation-State. Encyclopædia Britannica. https://www. britannica.com/topic/nation-state

Fleck, R. K., & Hanssen, F. A. (2013). How Tyranny Paved the Way to Democracy: The Democratic Transition in Ancient Greece. The Journal of Law and Economics. https://doi.org/10.1086/670731

Greene, J. P. (2000). The American Revolution. The American Historical Review. https://doi.org/10.2307/2652437

Gunderson, G. (1974). The Origin of the American Civil War. The Journal of Economic History. https://www.jstor.org/stable/2116615

History.com Editors. (2009, October 27). War of 1812. History Channel. https://www.history.com/topics/19th-century/war-of-1812

History.com Editors. (2018, April 4). Democratic Party. History. com. https://www.history.com/topics/us-government-and-politics/ democratic-party

History.com Editors. (2021, February 1). Republican Party. History. com. https://www.history.com/topics/us-government-and-politics/ republican-party

Hill, K. Q., & Leighley, J. E. (1996). Political Parties and Class Mobilization in Contemporary United States Elections. American Journal of Political Science. https://doi.org/10.2307/2111795

Joy, A. (2021, November 17). Why The U.S. Is "Already In An Authoritarian State. Intercessors for America. https://ifapray.org/blog/ why-the-u-s-is-already-in-an-authoritarian-state/

Kaiser, T. E. (1979). Feudalism and the French Revolution. The History Teacher. https://doi.org/10.2307/491982

Lane, M. (2015). The Birth of Politics. Princton University Press. https://doi.org/10.2307/j.ctvc7721z

Little, L. K. (2002). Monastism and Western Society: From Marginality to the Establishment and back. Memoirs of the American Academy in Rome. https://doi.org/10.2307/4238793

Meyer, A. G. (1977). Two Worlds: Communism and Western Society. Slavic Review. https://doi.org/10.2307/2494980

Norenzayan, A. (2006). Evolution and Transmitted Culture. Psychological Inquiry. https://www.jstor.org/stable/20447312

Oxley, Z. (2020). Framing and Political Decision Making: An Overview. Oxford Research Encyclopedia of Politics. https://doi.org/10.1093/acrefore/9780190228637.013.1250

Piperno, D. R. (2011). The Origins of Plant Cultivation and Domestication in the New World Tropics. Current Anthropology. https://doi.org/10.1086/659998

Riker, W. H. (1982). The Two-Party System and Duverger's Law: An Essay on the History of Political Science. The American Political Science Review, 76(4), 753. https://doi.org/10.2307/1962968

Rostker, B. (2013). The Civil War, In Providing for the Casualties of War: The American Experience Through World War II. RAND Corporation. http://www.jstor.org/stable/10.7249/j.ctt2tt90p.13

Studymode. (n.d.). Alexander Hamilton's Two-Party System. Studymode. com. https://www.studymode.com/essays/Alexander-Hamiltons-Two-Party-System-85895637.html

Thornton D. (2020, November 9). History of the Democratic and Republican Parties. The Heritage Herald. https://heritageherald. com/2020/11/09/history-of-the-democratic-and-republican-parties/

Wolchover, N. (2012, September 24). Why Did the Democratic and Republican Parties Switch Platforms. Live Science. https://www. livescience.com/34241-democratic-republican-parties-switch-platforms. html

Wollheim, R. (1958). Democracy. Journal of the History of Ideas. https://doi.org/10.2307/2707936

Chapter 3: Abortion

Abboud, C. (2017). Doe v. Bolton (1973).The Embryo Project Encyclopedia. Asu.edu. https://embryo.asu.edu/pages/doe-v-bolton-1973

ABC News (2022, June 24). Abortion in America: A Visual Timeline. ABC News. https://abcnews.go.com/Politics/abortion-america-visual-timeline/story?id=85588254

Acevedo, Z. (1979). Abortion in early America. Women & Health. https://doi.org/10.1300/j013v04n02_05

Arablouei, R. (2022, June 6). Abortion was once Common Practice in America. NPR. https://www.npr.org/2022/06/06/1103372543/abortion-was-once-common-practice-in-america-a-small-group-of-doctors-changed-th

Aron, N. R. (2022, July 26). The father of American gynecology fought to criminalize abortion in the 1850s. Medium. https://timeline.com/horatio-storer-criminal-abortion-c433606491da

Babic, I. & Richardson, E. (2022, June 24). Abortion in America: A Visual Timeline. ABC News. https://abcnews.go.com/Politics/abortion-america-visual-timeline/story?id=85588254

Bauer, P. (2017, April 3). Norma McCorvey Biography & Facts. Encyclopedia Britannica. https://www.britannica.com/biography/Norma-McCorvey

Berer, M. (2017). Abortion Law and Policy Around the World: In Search of Decriminalization. Health and Human Rights. https://www.jstor.org/stable/90007912

Betancourt, R. (2020, December 11). Abortion and contraception in the Middle Ages. Scientific American. https://www.scientificamerican.com/article/abortion-and-contraception-in-the-middle-ages/

Blakemore, E. (2022, June 23). The tumultuous history that led to the landmark Roe v. Wade ruling. History.com. https://www.nationalgeographic.com/history/article/roe-v-wade-the-tumultuous-history-that-led-to-the-landmark-ruling?loggedin=true&rnd=1692348341716

Blakemore, E. (2023, April 11). The complex early history of abortion in the United States. History.com. https://www.nationalgeographic.com/

history/article/the-complex-early-history-of-abortion-in-the-united-stat
es?rnd=1689496223544&loggedin=true

Britannica Editors. (2019). Democratic-Republican Party History &
Ideology. Encyclopædia Britannica. https://www.britannica.com/topic/
Democratic-Republican-Party

Childress, C. (2012). The Truth About Margaret Sanger. Blackgenocide.org.
http://www.blackgenocide.org/sanger.html

ERDMAN, J. N. (2017). Theorizing Time in Abortion Law and
Human Rights. Health and Human Rights. https://www.jstor.org/
stable/90007913

Hovey, G. (1985). Abortion: a history. Planned Parenthood Review. https://
pubmed.ncbi.nlm.nih.gov/12340403/

Hunt, K. (2023, June 23). Abortion is ancient history: Long before
Roe, women terminated pregnancies. CNN. https://www.cnn.
com/2023/06/23/health/abortion-is-ancient-history-and-that-matters-
today-scn/index.html

King, E. (2016, November 29). What Abortion Looked Like 1000
Years Ago. Vice.com. https://www.vice.com/en/article/4w358p/
what-abortion-looked-like-1000-years-ago

Klabusich, K. (2016, January 22). Abortion Is as Old as Pregnancy: 4,000
Years of Reproductive Rights. Truthout. https://truthout.org/articles/
abortion-is-as-old-as-pregnancy-4-000-years-of-reproductive-rights-
history/

Lim, S. (2022). Reproductive Rights in Georgia: Doe v. Bolton. Atlanta
History Center. https://www.atlantahistorycenter.com/blog/
reproductive-rights-in-georgia-doe-v-bolton/

Lohr, P. A., Fjerstad, M., DeSilva, U., & Lyus, R. (2014). Abortion. British
Medical Journal. https://www.jstor.org/stable/26511467

Lowen, M. (2022, June 25). Roe v Wade: The world reacts to US
abortion ruling. BBC News. https://www.bbc.com/news/
world-us-canada-61788929

Luisiana State University. (2019). Declaration of Death Lsu.edu. https://
biotech.law.lsu.edu/books/lbb/x553.htm

Minnesota Citizens Concerned for Life. (2019). Why Pro-Life? The Case
for Inclusion. MCCL.com https://www.mccl.org/whyprolife

Parker, H. (2014). Taking the Trade Timeline. Department of History University of Connecticut. https://history.uconn.edu/taking-the-trade-timeline/

Sommer, M. (2010, December) .Abortion in late Imperial China: Routine Birth Control or Crisis intervention? John Hopkins University Press/ Project Muse. https://www.buffalo.edu/content/dam/www/genderin/Sommer,%202010,%20Abortion%20in%20Late%20Imperial%20China.pdf

Teachme Surgery Team. (2017, August 28). How to Certify Death Examination Documentation. TeachMeSurgery. https://teachmesurgery.com/examinations/misc/confirmation-of-death/

The Editors of Encyclopaedia Britannica. (2023, August 16). Abortion Definition, Procedure, Laws, & Facts. Encyclopedia Britannica. https://www.britannica.com/science/abortion-pregnancy

The Editors of Encyclopaedia Britannica. (2023, August 16). Roe v. Wade Summary, Origins, & Influence. Encyclopedia Britannica. https://www.britannica.com/event/Roe-v-Wade

Venkatrama, R. (2020, September, 21). Horatio Robinson Storer (1830-1922). Embryo Project Encyclopedia. https://embryo.asu.edu/pages/horatio-robinson-storer-1830-1922

Wilkinson, K. (2023, August 22). Abortion Facts and Statistics: What You Need to Know. Verywell Health. https://www.verywellhealth.com/facts-about-abortion-5324508

Chapter 4: Marriage

Anderson, R. (2013, March 11). Marriage: What It Is, Why It Matters, and the Consequences of Redefining It. The Heritage Foundation. https://www.heritage.org/marriage-and-family/report/marriage-what-it-why-it-matters-and-the-consequences-redefining-it

Anderson, R. (2019). Why Is Government in the Marriage Business? The Heritage Foundation. https://www.heritage.org/marriage-and-family/commentary/why-government-the-marriage-business

Chamie, J. (2022, August 12). The End of Marriage in America. The Hill. https://thehill.com/opinion/finance/567107-the-end-of-marriage-in-america /

Daryanani, I., Hamilton, J. L., Abramson, L. Y., & Alloy, L. B. (2016). Single Mother Parenting and Adolescent Psychopathology. Journal of Abnormal Child Psychology. https://doi.org/10.1007/s10802-016-0128-x

Everitt, B. L. (2012, March 14). Ten key moments in the history of marriage. BBC News. https://www.bbc.com/news/magazine-17351133

Fagan, P. (1995, March 17). The Real Root Causes of Violent Crime: The Breakdown of Marriage, Family, and Community. The Heritage Foundation. https://www.heritage.org/crime-and-justice/report/the-real-root-causes-violent-crime-the-breakdown-marriage-family-and

Gavrilets, S. (2012). Human origins and the transition from promiscuity to pair-bonding. Proceedings of the National Academy of Sciences. https://doi.org/10.1073/pnas.1200717109

Goldman, N., Westoff, C. F., & Hammerslough, C. (1984). Demography of the Marriage Market in the United States. Population Index. https://doi.org/10.2307/2736903

Hafera, B. (2023, September 5). The Real Crisis Affecting the American Family | The Heritage Foundation. The Heritage Foundation. https://www.heritage.org/marriage-and-family/commentary/the-real-crisis-affecting-the-american-family

Josephs, L. (2019, April 14.). Is Monogamy Natural. Psychology Today. https://www.psychologytoday.com/us/blog/between-the-sheets/201904/is-monogamy-natural

Lundberg, S., & Pollak, R. A. (2015). The Evolving Role of Marriage: 1950-2010. The Future of Children. https://www.jstor.org/stable/43581971

Miranda-Ramos, M., & Vasconcelos, I. G. (2019). Paternity Certainty. Encyclopedia of Evolutionary Psychological Science. https://doi.org/10.1007/978-3-319-16999-6_129-1

Rector, R. (2014, November 17). How Welfare Undermines Marriage and What to Do About It. The Heritage Foundation. https://www.heritage.org/welfare/report/how-welfare-undermines-marriage-and-what-do-about-it

Sawhill, I. (2016, July 28). Are Children Raised With Absent Fathers Worse Off? Brookings. https://www.brookings.edu/articles/are-children-raised-with-absent-fathers-worse-off/

The Editors of Encyclopaedia Britannica. (2023, October 17). Marriage | Definition, History, Types, customs, Laws, & Facts. Encyclopedia Britannica. https://www.britannica.com/topic/marriage

Uecker, J. E., & Stokes, C. E. (2008). Early Marriage in the United States. Journal of Marriage and Family. https://www.jstor.org/stable/40056302

US Census Bureau. (2021, October 8). Number, timing and duration of marriages and divorces. Census.gov. https://www.census.gov/newsroom/press-releases/2021/marriages-and-divorces.html

US Census Bureau. (2022, July 6). Marriage and divorce. Census.gov. https://www.census.gov/topics/families/marriage-and-divorce.html

US Department of Treasury. (2023, November 15). The American Rescue Plan will deliver   immediate economic relief to families. U.S. Department of The Treasury. https://home.treasury.gov/news/featured-stories/fact-sheet-the-american-rescue-plan-will-deliver-immediate-economic-relief-to-families

United States Joint Economic Committee. (2020, April 29). U.S. marriage rates hit new recorded low. U.S. Marriage Rates Hit New Recorded Low. United States Joint Economic Committee. https://www.jec.senate.gov/public/index.cfm/republicans/2020/4/marriage-rate-blog-test

Wilcox, W. B. (2009). The evolution of divorce. National Affairs. https://www.nationalaffairs.com/publications/detail/the-evolution-of-divorce

Young, L. J. (2003). The Neural Basis of Pair Bonding in a Monogamous Species: A Model for Understanding the Biological Basis of Human Behavior. National Academies Press. https://www.ncbi.nlm.nih.gov/books/NBK97287/

Chapter 5: Transgenderism

Abel, B. S. (2014). Hormone Treatment of Children and Adolescents with Gender Dysphoria: An Ethical Analysis. The Hastings Center Report. https://www.jstor.org/stable/44159362

A brief history of "gender." (2016, December 28). Language: A Feminist Guide; language: a feminist guide. https://debuk.wordpress.com/2016/12/15/a-brief-history-of-gender/

Allen, J. (2022, June 10). New study estimates 1.6 million in U.S. identify as transgender. Reuters. https://www.reuters.com/world/us/new-study-estimates-16-million-us-identify-transgender-2022-06-10/

Beemyn, G & Schroth, L. (2014). Transgender History in the United States
A special unabridged version of a book chapter from Trans Bodies,
Trans Selves. Umass.edu https://www.umass.edu/stonewall/sites/
default/files/Infoforandabout/transpeople/genny_beemyn_transgender_
history_in_the_united_states.pdf

Blakemore, E. (2023, May 24). How historians are documenting
the lives of transgender people. National Geographic.
https://www.nationalgeographic.com/history/article/
how-historians-are-documenting-lives-of-transgender-people

Brooks, J. (2018, May 23). The Controversial Research on "Desistance" in
Transgender Youth. KQED. https://www.kqed.org/futureofyou/441784/
the-controversial-research-on-desistance-in-transgender-youth

Carmichael, P., Butler, G., Masic, U., Cole, T. J., De Stavola, B. L.,
Davidson, S., Skageberg, E. M., Khadr, S., & Viner, R. M. (2021).
Short-term outcomes of pubertal suppression in a selected cohort of
12 to 15 year old young people with persistent gender dysphoria in the
UK. *PLOS ONE, 16*(2), e0243894. https://doi.org/10.1371/journal.
pone.0243894

Cleveland Clinic. (2021, August 20). Genetic Disorders: What Are
They, Types, Symptoms & Causes. Cleveland Clinic. https://
my.clevelandclinic.org/health/diseases/21751-genetic-disorders

Dallenbach, K. M. (1956). Madison Bentley: 1870-1955. *The American
Journal of Psychology, 69*(2), 169–193. http://www.jstor.org/
stable/1418148

Dembroff, R. (2018). Real Talk on the Metaphysics of Gender.
Philosophical Topics. https://www.jstor.org/stable/26927949

Erickson-Schroth, L. (2014). Trans bodies, trans selves : a resource for the
transgender community. Oxford University Press.

Garg G, Elshimy G, Marwaha R. (2023, July 11). Gender Dysphoria.
University of Arizona/ National Library of Medicine. https://www.ncbi.
nlm.nih.gov/books/NBK532313 /

Ghorayshi, A. (2022, June 10). Report reveals sharp rise in transgender
young people in the U.S. The New York Times. https://www.nytimes.
com/2022/06/10/science/transgender-teenagers-national-survey.html

Illam, T. (2009) Transgenderism: Facts and fictions. National Library of Medicine/Indian Journal of Psychiatry. https://www.ncbi.nlm.nih.gov/pmc/articles/PMC2738402/

Kao, E. (2021, June 30). We'll Tell You What "60 Minutes+" Won't About How Transgender Movement Endangers Kids. The Heritage Foundation. https://www.heritage.org/gender/commentary/well-tell-you-what-60-minutes-wont-about-how-transgender-movement-endangers-kids

Lewis, D. C., Flores, A. R., Haider-Markel, D. P., Miller, P. R., Tadlock, B. L., & Taylor, J. K. (2017). Degrees of Acceptance: Variation in Public Attitudes toward Segments of the LGBT Community. Political Research Quarterly. https://www.jstor.org/stable/26384822

Mayo Clinic Staff. (2021, September 14). Pubertal blockers for transgender and gender diverse youth. Mayo Clinic. https://www.mayoclinic.org/diseases-conditions/gender-dysphoria/in-depth/pubertal-blockers/art-20459075

Mayo Clinic. (2022, February 26). Gender dysphoria - Symptoms and causes. Mayo Clinic. https://www.mayoclinic.org/diseases-conditions/gender-dysphoria/symptoms-causes/syc-20475255

Mitchell, T. (2022, June 28). Americans' Complex views on gender identity and transgender issues | Pew Research Center. Pew Research Center's Social & Demographic Trends Project. https://www.pewresearch.org/social-trends/2022/06/28/americans-complex-views-on-gender-identity-and-transgender-issues/

Money, J., & Ehrhardt, A. A. (1972). *Man and woman, boy and girl: Differentiation and dimorphism of gender identity from conception to maturity.* Johns Hopkins U. Press.

MONEY, J. (1957). Imprinting and the Establishment of Gender Role. *Archives of Neurology and Psychiatry, 77*(3), 333. https://doi.org/10.1001/archneurpsyc.1957.02330330119019

Money, J. (1955). Linguistic resources and psychodynamic theory. *British Journal of Medical Psychology, 28,* 264–266. https://doi.org/10.1111/j.2044-8341.1955.tb00900.x

Money, J., & Tucker, P. (1975). *Sexual signatures: On being a man or a woman.* Little, Brown.

Money, J. (1994). The Concept of gender identity disorder in childhood and adolescence after 39 years. *Journal of Sex & Marital Therapy, 20*(3), 163–177. https://doi.org/10.1080/00926239408403428

Stone, M. H. (1980). Traditional Psychoanalytic Characterology Reexamined in the Light of Constitutional and Cognitive Differences Between the Sexes. *Journal of the American Academy of Psychoanalysis, 8*(3), 381–401. https://doi.org/10.1521/jaap.1.1980.8.3.381

Whittle, S. (2010, June 2). A brief history of transgender issues. The Guardian. https://www.theguardian.com/lifeandstyle/2010/jun/02/brief-history-transgender-issues

Vincent, C. (2021, August 20). Transgenderism in ancient cultures. LGBT Health and Wellbeing. https://www.lgbthealth.org.uk/blog/transgenderism-in-ancient-cultures/

Chapter 6 Environmentalism

Babich, A. (2012). The Supremacy Clause, Cooperative Federalism, and the Full Federal Regulatory Purpose. Administrative Law Review. https://www.jstor.org/stable/23316180

Barnett, R. (N,D). Interpretation: The Commerce Clause. National Constitution Center constitutioncenter.org. https://constitutioncenter.org/the-constitution/articles/article-i/clauses/752

Birkby, R. H. (1966). Politics of Accommodation: The Origin of the Supremacy Clause. The Western Political Quarterly. https://doi.org/10.2307/445476

Charnovitz, S. (1993). The Environment Vs. Trade Rules: Defogging the Debate. Environmental Law. https://www.jstor.org/stable/43266057

Cornell Law School. (2018, September 18). Commerce Clause. Legal Information Institute. https://www.law.cornell.edu/wex/commerce_clause

Da Mata, J., Mesquita, A., & Neto, R. (2017). *COMPARISON OF THE PERFORMANCE, ADVANTAGES AND DISADVANTAGES OF NUCLEAR POWER GENERATION COMPARED TO OTHER CLEAN SOURCES OF ELECTRICITY.* https://inis.iaea.org/collection/NCLCollectionStore/_Public/49/009/49009723.pdf?r=1

Dietz, T., Duan, R., Nalley, J., & Van Witsen, A. (2018). Social Support for Water Quality: The Influence of Values and Symbolic Racism. Human Ecology Review. https://www.jstor.org/stable/26506661

Donnelly, W. H. (1965). Nuclear Power and Merchant Shipping. In *Google Books*. U.S. Atomic Energy Commission, Division of Technical Information. https://books.google.com/books?hl=en&lr=&id=5ShjcSgn vF0C&oi=fnd&pg=PA1&dq=nuclear+ships+merchant&ots=pN1lylqa HF&sig=rq354qYAtlaP4FNHPtDCS_Q2aNg

Elliott, L. (1998, July 20). Environmentalism | Ideology, History, & Types. Encyclopedia Britannica. https://www.britannica.com/topic/ environmentalism

Freire, L. O., & Andrade, D. A. de. (2015). Historic survey on nuclear merchant ships. *Nuclear Engineering and Design, 293*, 176–186. https:// doi.org/10.1016/j.nucengdes.2015.07.031

Graves, C., Ebbesen, S. D., Mogensen, M., & Lackner, K. S. (2011). Sustainable hydrocarbon fuels by recycling CO_2 and H_2O with renewable or nuclear energy. *Renewable and Sustainable Energy Reviews, 15*(1), 1–23. https://doi.org/10.1016/j.rser.2010.07.014

Holst, A. (2017, January 4). Clean Air Act (CAA) | History & Effects. Encyclopedia Britannica. https://www.britannica.com/topic/ Clean-Air-Act-United-States-1970

History.com Editors. (2017, October 6). Climate Change History. History. https://www.history.com/topics/natural-disasters-and-environment/ history-of-climate-change

Irfan, U. (2020, January 17). 21 kids sued the government over climate change. A federal court dismissed the case. Vox. https://www.vox.com/2020/1/17/21070810/ climate-change-lawsuit-juliana-vs-us-our-childrens-trust-9th-circuit

Jones, C. M. (2018). Deciding on the Future: Comparing the Environmental and Economic Advantages of Renewable Energy and Nuclear Power. *Scholarspace.manoa.hawaii.edu*. https://scholarspace. manoa.hawaii.edu/items/acf6a488-f37e-4468-8bb8-0d954c8194cc

Joselow, M. (2021, September 29). Biden officials finalize a rule making it harder to kill birds, reversing Trump. Washington Post. https:// www.washingtonpost.com/climate-environment/2021/09/29/ migratory-bird-treaty-act-biden

Keer, T. (2023). Understanding the Migratory Bird Treaty Act of 1918. Wildfowl. https://www.wildfowlmag.com/editorial/understanding-migratory-bird-treaty-act-1918/473606

Krier, J. E. (1986) Environmental Regulation and the Constitution. Encyclopedia.com. https://www.encyclopedia.com/politics/encyclopedias-almanacs-transcripts-and-maps/environmental-regulation-and-constitution

Krosofsky, A. (2021, February 2). Why Are Rising Sea Levels a Bad Thing for Humanity's Future? Green Matters. https://www.greenmatters.com/p/why-sea-level-rise-bad#:~:text=There%20are%20quite%20a%20few%20reasons

Lindsey, R., & Dahlman, L. (2023, January 18). Climate Change: Global Temperature. Climate.Gov. https://www.climate.gov/news-features/understanding-climate/climate-change-global-temperature

Mann, M. E. (2019). Global Warming. Encyclopedia Britannica. https://www.britannica.com/science/global-warming

Merriam-Webster Dictionary. (2023). Definition of environmentalism. Merriam-Webster Dictionary. https://www.merriam-webster.com/dictionary/environmentalism

Moore, S. (2017, July 14). Why the Greens Hate Nuclear Power. The Heritage Foundation. https://www.heritage.org/nuclear-energy/commentary/why-the-greens-hate-nuclear-power

Nasa. (n.d.). The Causes of Climate Change. Nasa. https://climate.nasa.gov/causes/?ref-hir.harvard.edu

Ozimek, A. (2017, February 26). Why I Don't Support Open Borders. Forbes. https://www.forbes.com/sites/modeledbehavior/2017/02/26/why-i-dont-support-open-borders/?sh=3dbae58f7b61

Public Broadcasting Service. (2017, June 2). The modern environmental movement. PBS. https://www.pbs.org/wgbh/americanexperience/features/earth-days-modern-environmental-movement/

Ramey, J. (2018, October 23). Are EV battery plants creating more pollution than EVs eliminate. Autoweek. https://www.autoweek.com/news/green-cars/a1709966/will-some-gas-and-diesel-cars-still-produce-less-pollution-evs/

Ritchie, H. (2020, October 6). Cars, planes, trains: Where Do CO2 Emissions from Transport Come from? Our World in Data. https://ourworldindata.org/co2-emissions-from-transport

Singer, P. (2023, February 22). Environmental ethics | Definition, Examples, Future Generations, & Facts. Encyclopedia Britannica. https://www.britannica.com/topic/environmental-ethics-philosophy

Schmalensee, R. & Stavins, R. N. (2019). Policy Evolution under the Clean Air Act. The Journal of Economic Perspectives. https://www.jstor.org/stable/26796835

Schofer, E., & Granados, F. J. (2006). Environmentalism, Globalization and National Economies, 1980-2000. Social Forces. https://www.jstor.org/stable/4494946

The advantages and Disadvantages of Synthesizing of Arylarsonic Acids The advantages and Disadvantages of Synthesizing f Arylarsonic Acids The advantages and Disadvantages of Synthesizing. (2020). *International Journal of Pharmaceutical Research, 12*(1). https://doi.org/10.31838/ijpr/2020.12.01.154

The Editors of Encyclopaedia Britannica. (1998, July 20). Commerce clause | Examples, Importance, Cases, Dormant, & Definition. Encyclopedia Britannica. https://www.britannica.com/money/topic/commerce-clause

The Library of Congress (1951). U.S. Reports: Dyer v. Sims, 341 U.S. 22. The Library of Congress. https://www.loc.gov/item/usrep341022/

The US Environmental Protection Agency. (2023, June 27). Environmental Justice Timeline. US EPA. https://www.epa.gov/environmentaljustice/environmental-justice-timeline

Us Congress. (1787). U.S. Constitution. Library of Congress. https://constitution.congress.gov/constitution/

Chapter 7: Immigration

Abramitzky, R., & Boustan, L. (2017). Immigration in American Economic History. Journal of Economic Literature. https://doi.org/10.2307/26417159

Baxter, A. & Nowrasteh A. (2021, August 3). A Brief History of U.S. Immigration Policy from the Colonial Period to the Present Day. Cato Institute. https://www.cato.org/policy-analysis/brief-history-us-immigration-policy-colonial-period-present-day

Brookings.(2016) The Cost an Benefits of Immigration. Brookings. https://www.brookings.edu/wp-content/uploads/2016/07/braingain_chapter.pdf

Chamie, J. (2023, March 16) America is abandoning rationality to justify illegal immigration. The Hill. https://thehill.com/opinion/immigration/3903719-america-is-abandoning-rationality-to-justify-illegal-immigration/

Cohn, D. (2015, September 30). How U.S. immigration laws and rules have changed through history. Pew Research Center. https://www.pewresearch.org/short-reads/2015/09/30/how-u-s-immigration-laws-and-rules-have-changed-through-history/

Davis, H. (2023, March 14). Fighting Human Trafficking and Battling Biden's Open Border. The Heritage Foundation. https://www.heritage.org/immigration/commentary/fighting-human-trafficking-and-battling-bidens-open-border

Dwinell, E. (2023, February 17). Shocking Cost of the Illegal Immigration Crisis to Americans. The Heritage Foundation. https://www.heritage.org/immigration/commentary/shocking-cost-the-illegal-immigration-crisis-americans

Goodman, A. (2015). Nation of Migrants, Historians of Migration. Journal of American Ethnic History. https://doi.org/10.5406/jamcrethnhist.34.4.0007

Hankinson, S. (2023, October 6). The BorderLine: The Border Crisis by the Numbers. The Heritage Foundation. https://www.heritage.org/immigration/commentary/the-borderline-the-border-crisis-the-numbers

Hernandez, K. L. (2009). Mexican Immigration to the United States. OAH Magazine of History. https://www.jstor.org/stable/40506011

History.com Editors. (2009, October 29). U.S. immigration before 1965. HISTORY Channel. https://www.history.com/topics/immigration/u-s-immigration-before-1965

Hutchinson, M. (2009). Securing the Borders: Debating Immigration Policy in U.S. History. OAH Magazine of History. https://www.jstor.org/stable/40506015

Kamarck, E. and Stenglein, C. (2023, June 22). How many undocumented immigrants are in the United States and who are they? Brookings. https://www.brookings.edu/articles/

how-many-undocumented-immigrants-are-in-the-united-states-and-who-are-they/

Parry, S. (2018). Immigration. Encyclopedia Britannica. https://www.britannica.com/topic/immigration

Pew Research Center. (2023, November 21). Key findings about U.S. immigrants. Pew Research Center. https://www.pewresearch.org/short-reads/2020/08/20/key-findings-about-u-s-immigrants/

Shaw, A. (2023, March 8). Illegal immigration now costs US taxpayers $151 billion a year, new study finds. Fox News. https://www.foxnews.com/politics/illegal-immigration-costs-us-taxpayers-151-billion-year-study-finds

Shoichet, C. (2023, May 6). On this day 141 years ago, a new law began reshaping America. More than a century later, Congress apologized for it. CNN. https://www.cnn.com/2023/05/06/us/chinese-exclusion-act-1882-cec/index.html

Stimson, C. (2023, October 23). Preserving Due Process and the Rule of Law: Examining the Status of Our Nation's Immigration Courts. The Heritage Foundation. https://www.heritage.org/testimony/preserving-due-process-and-the-rule-law-examining-the-status-our-nations-immigration

Wallenfeldt, J. (2023, November 13). DACA | Meaning, Requirements, Renewal, & Dreamers. Encyclopedia Britannica. https://www.britannica.com/topic/DACA

Chapter 8: War

Cordesman, A. H. (2016). The Human Cost of War in the Middle East: A Graphic Overview. Center for Strategic and International Studies. https://www.jstor.org/stable/resrep23380

Dyson, S. B., & Parent, M. J. (2017). The operational code approach to profiling political leaders: understanding Vladimir Putin. Intelligence & National Security. https://doi.org/10.1080/02684527.2017.1313523

Fearon, J. D. (1995) Rationalist Explanations for War. The MIT Press. https://web.stanford.edu/group/fearon-research/cgi-bin/wordpress/wp-content/uploads/2013/10/Rationalist-Explanations-for-War.pdf

Fitzgerald, M., & Davis, E., Jr. (2023, July 25). Russia invades Ukraine: A timeline of the crisis. US News & World

Report. https://www.usnews.com/news/best-countries/
slideshows/a-timeline-of-the-russia-ukraine-conflict

Gaub, F. (2017). Arab Wars: calculating the costs. European Union Institute
for Security Studies. https://www.jstor.org/stable/resrep17445

Haglund, D. G. (2023, November 21). North Atlantic Treaty Organization
History, Structure & Purpose. Encyclopedia Britannica. https://www.
britannica.com/topic/North-Atlantic-Treaty-Organization

Khorram-Manesh, A., Burkle, F. M., Goniewicz, K., & Robinson, Y.
(2021). Estimating the Number of Civilian Casualties in Modern
Armed Conflicts-A Systematic Review. Frontiers in public health.
https://doi.org/10.3389/fpubh.2021.765261

Kimball, J. (2021, September 1). Costs of the 20-year war on terror: $8
trillion and 900,000 deaths. Brown University. https://www.brown.
edu/news/2021-09-01/costsofwar

Knickmeyer, E. (2021, August 17). Costs of the Afghanistan war,
in lives and dollars. AP News. https://apnews.com/article/
middle-east-business-afghanistan-43d8f53b35e80ec18c130cd683e1a38f

Kristian, B. (2017, February 1). American Taxpayers Must Be Told the Real
Cost of War. Forbes. https://www.forbes.com/sites/realspin/2017/02/01/
american-taxpayers-must-be-told-the-real-cost-of-war/

Knickmeyer, E. (2021, August 17). Costs of the Afghanistan war,
in lives and dollars. AP News. https://apnews.com/article/
middle-east-business-afghanistan-43d8f53b35e80ec18c130cd683e1a38f

Macias, A. (2019, November 20). America has spent $6.4 trillion on wars in
the Middle East and Asia since 2001, a new study says. CNBC. https://
www.cnbc.com/2019/11/20/us-spent-6point4-trillion-on-middle-east-
wars-since-2001-study.html

Sostaric, M. (2019). The American Wartime Propaganda During World
War II. Australasian Journal of American Studies. https://doi.
org/10.2307/26926687

Statista. (2023, October 12). How many nuclear bombs are there in the
world 2023. Statista. https://www.statista.com/statistics/264435/
number-of-nuclear-warheads-worldwide/

Statista. (2023, November 16). Civilian deaths in Iraq war 2003-
2023. Statista. https://www.statista.com/statistics/269729/
documented-civilian-deaths-in-iraq-war-since-2003/

Stevens, B., & Hellyer, M. (2022). The cost of war. Australian Strategic Policy Institute. http://www.jstor.org/stable/resrep41999.11

U.S. Department of Defense. (n.d.). Support for Ukraine: Timeline. US DOD. https://www.defense.gov/Spotlights/Support-for-Ukraine/Timeline/

US House of Representatives: History, Art & Archives. (n.d.). Power to Declare War. History.House.gov. https://history.house.gov/Institution/Origins-Development/War-Powers/

Chapter 9: Guns

Carlson, J., Harel Shapira, & Goss, K. A. (2019). *Gun studies : interdisciplinary approaches to politics, policy, and practice.* Routledge.

Charles, P. J. (2017). Second Amendment | Contents, Supreme Court Interpretations, & History. In *Encyclopædia Britannica.* https://www.britannica.com/topic/Second-Amendment

Ciocchetti, C. (2013). 2nd Amendment: The Right to Keep & Bear Arms -- Teaching D.C. v. Heller. *SSRN Electronic Journal.* https://doi.org/10.2139/ssrn.2270397

Constitution Annotated. (n.d.). *Second Amendment | Browse | Constitution Annotated | Congress.gov | Library of Congress.* Constitution.congress.gov. https://constitution.congress.gov/browse/amendment-2/

Dowlut, R. (1989). *The 2nd Amendment: To Keep and Bear Arms.* Social Science Research Network. https://ssrn.com/abstract=2549244

Founding Fathers Quotes on Guns and the Right to Keep and Bear Arms in the Second Amendment. (n.d.). Ammo.com. https://ammo.com/articles/founding-fathers-quotes-second-amendment-guns-keep-and-bear-arms

Gerry, E. (1789, August 17). *Debate over the Second Amendment, I Annals of Congress at 750.* Millitary Dispatch.com. https://www.militiadispatch.com/history-law/

Guha, B. (2013). Guns and crime revisited. *Journal of Economic Behavior & Organization, 94,* 1–10. https://doi.org/10.1016/j.jebo.2013.07.019

Hagstrom, A. (2022, December 15). *CDC removed stats on defensive gun use over pressure from gun control activists: report.* Fox News. https://www.foxnews.com/politics/cdc-removed-stats-defensive-gun-use-pressure-gun-control-activists-report

History.com Editors. (2018, August 21). *Bill of Rights*. HISTORY. https://www.history.com/topics/united-states-constitution/bill-of-rights

History.com Editors. (2017, December 4). *The Second Amendment - Definition, text & rights. HISTORY.com*. https://www.history.com/topics/united-states-constitution/2nd-amendment

History.com Editors. (2018, August 21). *Second Amendment*. HISTORY; A&E Television Networks. https://www.history.com/topics/united-states-constitution/2nd-amendment

Hsiao, T. (2021, October 5). *Guns used more for self-defense than crimes*. The Washington Times. https://www.washingtontimes.com/news/2021/oct/5/guns-used-more-for-self-defense-than-crimes/

Kaur, H. (2022, June 2). *What studies reveal about gun ownership in the U.S.* CNN. https://www.cnn.com/2022/06/02/us/gun-ownership-numbers-us-cec/index.html

Kessler, G. (2021, June 28). *Biden's false claim that the 2nd Amendment bans cannon ownership*. Washington Post. https://www.washingtonpost.com/politics/2021/06/28/bidens-false-claim-that-2nd-amendment-bans-cannon-ownership/

Legal Information Institute. (n.d.). *Second Amendment*. Legal Information Institute. https://www.law.cornell.edu/wex/second_amendment

Lott, Jr., J. R. (2001). Guns, Crime, and Safety: Introduction. *The Journal of Law and Economics, 44*(S2), 605–614. https://doi.org/10.1086/341243

Lott, J.R. (2010, May 24). *More Guns Less Crime Understanding Crime and Gun Control Laws, Third Edition*. University of Chicago Press. 242477

Ludwig, J., & Lott, J. R. (1999). More Guns, Less Crime: Understanding Crime and Gun Control Laws. *Contemporary Sociology, 28*(4), 466. https://doi.org/10.2307/2655341

Martinell, T., & Martinell, T. (2018, December 29). *What does the word "Arms" mean in the 2nd Amendment? | Tenth Amendment Center*. Tenth Amendment Center. https://tenthamendmentcenter.com/2016/06/30/what-does-the-word-arms-mean-in-the-2nd-amendment/

McPhedran, S. (2013). More guns … more or less crime? An Australian perspective on an international question. *Crime Prevention and Community Safety, 15*(2), 127–133. https://doi.org/10.1057/cpcs.2012.17

Megan E. Collins, Susan T. Parker, Thomas L. Scott, & Charles F. Wellford. (2017). A Comparative Analysis of Crime Guns. *RSF: The Russell Sage Foundation Journal of the Social Sciences*, *3*(5), 96. https://doi.org/10.7758/rsf.2017.3.5.05

Moody, C. E., & Marvell, T. B. (2005). Guns and Crime. *Southern Economic Journal*, *71*(4), 720–736. https://doi.org/10.1002/j.2325-8012.2005.tb00672.x

Nra-Ila. (n.d.). *NRA-ILA | What Is The Second Amendment And How Is It Defined*. NRA-ILA. https://www.nraila.org/what-is-the-second-amendment-and-how-is-it-defined/

Second Amendment: Doctrine and Practice. (n.d.). LII / Legal Information Institute. https://www.law.cornell.edu/constitution-conan/amendment-2/second-amendment-doctrine-and-practice

Second Amendment. (2017, October 10). LII / Legal Information Institute. https://www.law.cornell.edu/constitution/second_amendment

Statista. (2023, June 2). *Gun ownership in the U.S. 1972-2022*. Statista. https://www.statista.com/statistics/249740/percentage-of-households-in-the-united-states-owning-a-firearm/

Stolzenberg, L., & D'Alessio, S. J. (2000). Gun Availability and Violent Crime: New Evidence from the National Incident-Based Reporting System. *Social Forces*, *78*(4), 1461. https://doi.org/10.2307/3006181

The Editors of Encyclopedia Britannica. (2019). Bill of Rights | Definition, Origins, Contents, & Application to the States. In *Encyclopædia Britannica*. https://www.britannica.com/topic/Bill-of-Rights-United-States-Constitution

The Wasington Standard. (2020, July 1). *Founding Fathers Quotes on Guns & the Second Amendment's Right to Keep & Bear Arms*. The Washington Standard. https://thewashingtonstandard.com/founding-fathers-quotes-on-guns-the-second-amendments-right-to-keep-bear-arms/

T. M. M. (2016, June 30). *What Does the Word "Arms" Mean in the 2nd Amendment? | | Tenth Amendment Center*. Tenthamendmentcenter.com. https://tenthamendmentcenter.com/2016/06/30/what-does-the-word-arms-mean-in-the-2nd-amendment/

Smith, M. L. (2014). The Second Amendment Implications of Regulating 3D Printed Firearms. *SSRN Electronic Journal*. https://doi.org/10.2139/ssrn.2401563

Sullum, J. (2022, September 9). *Defensive firearms use is common, Largest-Ever Survey of U.S. gun Owners finds.* Reason.com. https://reason.com/2022/09/09/the-largest-ever-survey-of-american-gun-owners-finds-that-defensive-use-of-firearms-is-common/

Swearer, A. (2019, February 12). *The Role of Mental Illness in Mass Shootings, Suicides.* The Heritage Foundation. https://www.heritage.org/public-health/commentary/the-role-mental-illness-mass-shootings-suicides

Washington, G. (1780, January 29). *Founders online: From George Washington to Elbridge Gerry.* University of Virginia Press. https://founders.archives.gov/documents/Washington/03-24-02-0242

Wright, J. D., Peter Henry Rossi, Daly, K., & Weber, E. (2006). *Under the gun: weapons, crime, and violence in America.* Aldine Transaction.

Zimring, F. E. (1975). Firearms and Federal Law: The Gun Control Act of 1968. *The Journal of Legal Studies,* 4(1), 133–198. https://doi.org/10.1086/467528

Chapter 10: Welfare

AP News. (2020, October 27). Trump administration proposes reversal of homeless policy. AP News. https://apnews.com/article/donald-trump-united-states-homelessness-cb42464c68d45ec7e1123f0ab19f8024

Bayba, M. (2023). How Do You Measure the True Success of Drug Rehab Programs. Addiction Group. https://www.addictiongroup.org/resources/faq/effective/

Begody, C. (2023, April 10). Fifty important statistics on welfare in 2023. Lexington Law. https://www.lexingtonlaw.com/blog/finance/welfare-statistics.html

Brooks, K. J. (2023, June 21). The homelessness population in major U.S. cities is on the rise. CBS News. https://www.cbsnews.com/news/federal-homelessness-statistics-us-2023-data/

Burt, M. (1992). Over the Edge: The Growth of Homelessness in the 1980's. Russell Sage Foundation. http://www.jstor.org/stable/10.7758/9781610440998

Chantrill, C. (2020, December 6). Analysis of recent US welfare spending. US Spending. https://www.usgovernmentspending.com/welfare_spending

Engel, P. (2018, October 26). General Welfare Clause. The Constitution Study. https://constitutionstudy.com/2018/10/26/general-welfare-clause/

Food Research Action Center. (2023, January 25). New USDA Report Provides Picture of Who Participates in SNAP. Food Research & Action Center. https://frac.org/blog/new-usda-report-provides-picture-of-who-participates-in-snap

Garfinkel, I., & Piliavin, I. (1995). Trends in the Size of the Nation's Homeless Population during the 1980s: A Surprising Result. Institute for Research on Poverty. https://www.irp.wisc.edu/publications/dps/pdfs/dp103494.pdf

Greenslade B. (2010, August 13). Is Social Security Constitutional. Tenth Amendment Center. https://tenthamendmentcenter.com/2010/08/13/is-social-security-constitutional/

Hall, L., & Nchako, C. (2023). A Closer Look at Who Benefits from SNAP: State-by-State Fact Sheets. Center on Budget and Policy Priorities. https://www.cbpp.org/research/a-closer-look-at-who-benefits-from-snap-state-by-state-fact-sheets#Alabama

Haskins, Ron. (2016, July 28). The War on Poverty: What went wrong? Brookings https://www.brookings.edu/articles/the-war-on-poverty-what-went-wrong/

Heilman, G. (2022, January 22). How much is a monthly welfare check Diario AS. https://en.as.com/en/2022/01/22/latest_news/1642820139_262174.html

History Channel Editors. (2009, October 29). New deal - programs, social security & FDR. History.com. https://www.history.com/topics/great-depression/new-deal

Invisible People TV. (2022, October 9). History Of Homelessness. Invisible People TV. https://invisiblepeople.tv/history-of-homelessness/

Matthews, D. (2021, March 10). Biden stimulus: How Covid relief checks could reduce child poverty in the US. Vox. https://www.vox.com/policy-and-politics/22319572/joe-biden-american-rescue-plan-war-on-poverty

McCarthy, N. (2021, April 16). The Development of America's Homeless Population. Statista Infographics. https://www.statista.com/chart/24642/total-number-of-homeless-people-in-the-us-by-year/

Meyer, J. (2022, July 27). Trump is right about homelessness. Forbes. https://www.forbes.com/sites/jaredmeyer/2022/07/27/trump-is-right-about-homelessness/?sh=76db2812487a

Miller, J. (2023, April 28). Addiction & Homelessness - Statistics by age, race and gender. AddictionHelp.com. https://www.addictionhelp.com/addiction/homelessness/

National Academies of Sciences, Engineering, and Medicine. (2018, July 11). The History of Homelessness in the United States. National Library of Medicine; National Academies Press (US). https://www.ncbi.nlm.nih.gov/books/NBK519584/

National Alliance to End Homelessness. (2018, October 18). Ending chronic homelessness Saves taxpayers money. National Alliance to End Homelessness. https://endhomelessness.org/resource/ending-chronic-homelessness-saves-taxpayers-money-2/

National Institute of Mental Health. (2023, March). Mental illness. National Institute of Mental Health. https://www.nimh.nih.gov/health/statistics/mental-illness

National Alliance to End Homelessness. (2023, May 23). State of Homelessness: 2023 Edition. National Alliance to End Homelessness. https://endhomelessness.org/homelessness-in-america/homelessness-statistics/state-of-homelessness/

Pilon, M. (2018, August 29). How Bill Clinton's welfare reform changed America. HISTORY Channel. https://www.history.com/news/clinton-1990s-welfare-reform-facts

Raphelson, S. (2017, November 30). How The Loss Of U.S. Psychiatric Hospitals Led To A Mental Health Crisis. NPR. https://www.npr.org/2017/11/30/567477160/how-the-loss-of-u-s-psychiatric-hospitals-led-to-a-mental-health-crisis

Rector, R. (2021, November 8). Largest Welfare Increase in U.S. History Will Boost Government Support to $76,400 per Poor Family. The Heritage Foundation. https://www.heritage.org/welfare/report/largest-welfare-increase-us-history-will-boost-government-support-76400-poor-family

Rossi, P. H. (1990). The old homeless and the new homelessness in historical perspective. The American Psychologist. https://doi.org/10.1037//0003-066x.45.8.954

Roth, A. (2021, May 25). The truth about deinstitutionalization. The Atlantic. https://www.theatlantic.com/health/archive/2021/05/truth-about-deinstitutionalization/618986/

Stiker, H. (2013, November 7). Deinstitutionalization Mental health, social reintegration & policy implications. Encyclopedia Britannica. https://www.britannica.com/topic/deinstitutionalization

Social Security Administration. (2023,) Social Security Fact sheet. Social Security Administration. https://www.ssa.gov/news/press/factsheets/basicfact-alt.pdf

Substance Abuse and Mental Health Service Administration. (2011). Hrc Factsheet Current Statistics Prevalence Characteristics Homelessness. SAMHSA. https://www.samhsa.gov/sites/default/files/programs_campaigns/homelessness_programs_resources/hrc-factsheet-current-statistics-prevalence-characteristics-homelessness.pdf

Substance Abuse and Mental Health Services Administration (SAMHSA). (2023, January 4). SAMHSA announces National Survey on Drug Use and Health (NSDUH) results detailing mental illness and substance use levels in 2021. HHS.gov. https://www.hhs.gov/about/news/2023/01/04/samhsa-announces-national-survey-drug-use-health-results-detailing-mental-illness-substance-use-levels-2021.html

The Administration for Children and Familes. (2023, February 6) Characteristics and Financial Circumstances of TANF Recipients, Fiscal Year 2020. https://www.acf.hhs.gov/ofa/data/characteristics-and-financial-circumstances-tanf-recipients-fiscal-year-2020

Terilizzi, Emily and Norris Tina. (2021, October). Mental Health Treatment Among Adults: United States, 2020. Center of Disease Control. https://www.cdc.gov/nchs/data/databriefs/db419.pdf

The US Department of Housing and Urban Development.. (2023, November 7). HUD announces $2.8 billion in annual funding to help people. U.S. Department of Housing And Urban Development (HUD). https://www.hud.gov/press/press_releases_media_advisories/hud_no_23_062

Us Department of Housing and Urban Development. (2023, March 31). HUD announces $2.8 billion in annual funding to help people. U.S. Department of Housing and Urban Development. https://www.hud.gov/press/press_releases_media_advisories/hud_no_23_062

USA Facts. (2023, May 23). How many homeless people are in the US? What does the data miss? – USAFacts.com. https://usafacts.org/articles/how-many-homeless-people-are-in-the-us-what-does-the-data-miss/

White House. (2010, June 17). Opening doors.Whitehouse. gov. https://obamawhitehouse.archives.gov/blog/2010/06/15/obama-administration-unveil-national-strategic-plan-prevent-and-end-homelessness

Weiner G. (2016). A Constitutional Welfare State. Nationalaffairs. https://nationalaffairs.com/publications/detail/a-constitutional-welfare-state

West, T. G. (2015, May 19). Poverty and Welfare in the American Founding | The Heritage Foundation. The Heritage Foundation. https://www.heritage.org/poverty-and-inequality/report/poverty-and-welfare-the-american-founding

About the Authors

Alexander Oakes is a Marine Corps combat veteran with a BA in Political Science and an MA in Political Psychology. He is currently pursuing his PhD in Clinical Psychology at Arizona State University while he writes for The Mises Institute, Human Events, and 

The Thinking Conservative. He is also beginning to produce video content on all social media platforms (X, YouTube, Spotify, Rumble, etc.) under the handle @authoralexoakes.

Zachariah Oakes is a Marine Corps combat veteran and a current student at Arizona State University. He is also a firearms enthusiast, outspoken patriot, and an all-around a pretty neat guy.